NAPOLEON'S PRISONER
A Country Parson's Ten-Year Detention in France

John Parry-Wingfield

ARTHUR H. STOCKWELL LTD
Torrs Park   Ilfracombe   Devon
Established 1898
www.ahstockwell.co.uk

ISBN 978-0-7223-4152-0
Printed in Great Britain by
Arthur H. Stockwell Ltd
Torrs Park   Ilfracombe
Devon

CONTENTS

PREFACE

The Reverend Lancelot Charles Lee, who was a distant cousin of mine, wrote the letters in this book to his first cousin, Harry Lancelot Lee, between 1803 and 1812, when he was a *détenu*, or civilian prisoner, in Napoleon's France, mainly at Verdun. He was eventually released in 1814.

There are twenty-eight letters in all, which must be a small proportion of his output, since it is evident from these letters that he was a prolific letter-writer. However, they are sufficient to give a lively and colourful picture of both the man himself and the ups and downs of life as a *détenu*. Some of the set-piece descriptions – for example, of the horse races and theatricals and of his time in Paris – bring his experiences vividly to life.

In the Introduction I include details of Lee's life and set out the background to the world of the *détenus* in Verdun.

John Parry-Wingfield, 2012

INTRODUCTION

The Napoleonic Wars

On 25 March 1802, Britain and France signed the Treaty of Amiens, marking the end of the first phase of the Napoleonic Wars, which had started in 1793. The peace was to last little more than a year. Claiming that the British had breached its terms, Napoleon abrogated the treaty on 18 May 1803 and hostilities resumed, continuing until Napoleon's defeat at the Battle of Waterloo in 1815.

One consequence of the signing of the treaty was that the British were permitted to visit France for the first time in nearly ten years. They swarmed across the Channel in the summer and autumn of 1802 – peers, businessmen, doctors, scholars, artists and many others, as well as their servants and grooms and also criminals escaping justice. Most were curious to see the changes that had taken place in France following the 1789 revolution and the rise of Napoleon.

Amongst these tourists were Charles James Fox, the Whig statesman, who was invited to dinner by Napoleon in Paris; the artist J. M. W. Turner, who filled several sketchbooks; and William Hazlitt, the writer. An industrial exhibition of French products in the courtyard of the Louvre attracted many visitors. Another attraction was the 'Four Horsemen of the Apocalypse' sculpture, which had been looted from St Mark's in Venice during the French invasion of Italy.

With the abrogation of the Treaty of Amiens this happy interlude came to an end, and on 23 May 1803 the French Government passed a decree ordering all Britons in France between the ages of eighteen and sixty to be detained. The French excuse for this high-handed act was that all adults were candidates for military service and might become belligerents, not least if the projected invasion of Britain were to take place. In British eyes this was a lamentable extension of the rules of warfare – the first example of internment of civilians. There was no such internment of French civilians in Britain.

These internees were known as *détenus*. Estimates of their number vary widely between 800 and 10,000. One such *détenu* was the Reverend Lancelot Charles Lee, who had travelled to France for reasons of health. Like many others, he was to be detained in France for eleven years, until 1814.

Verdun: Centre for the *Détenus*

Lee, like very many of the civilian *détenus*, was held mainly at Verdun, which was where most of the prisoners of war of officer rank (mainly naval) were also detained. Some had wives and children with them. The total number varied over the years between 600 and 1,100.

Verdun was then a small fortified town of some 10,000 inhabitants on the banks of the River Meuse, the fortifications having been designed by the famous military engineer, Vauban. The junior prisoners of war were held in the military barracks and an old convent in the citadel; the officers and civilians were able to take lodgings in the town on parole, the quality of lodgings depending on the length of the prisoner's purse.

Described by one as 'a very dismal place; the inhabitants make but a sorry appearance', Verdun was transformed by the arrival of the British, many of them of ample means. Their arrival 'gave an air of importance to the depot and caused a

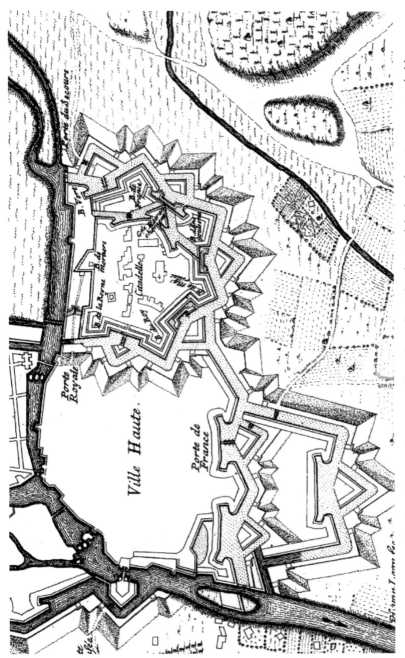

1695 print of Verdun showing the town walls and, on the right, the citadel where the prisoners were held. From Wikipedia.

circulation of fashion and splendour rarely to be met with even in watering places in England'.

According to another, 'Verdun soon began to lose the appearance of a French town; many shops with English signs were opened, such as "Anderson, Grocer and Tea Dealer from London," "Stuckey, Tailor and Ladies Habit Maker from London" etc. The Rue Moselle, the principal street, acquired the nom de guerre of Bond Street and was often called by the French "Bon Street."' Another writer observed: 'In the shops were to be found the most delicate and expensive of viands from the most distant provinces of the Empire; the celebrated pâté de foie gras, the poularde aux truffles of Paris, the oysters of Concarle and the tunny fish of the Mediterranean.' But not all could enjoy this luxury; many suffered hardship and deprivation.

Freedom of Movement: Escape

The *détenus* were at liberty to move round the town of Verdun and on the ramparts, but were required to report for *appel* at the Hotel de Ville (Town Hall) twice a day, at 10 a.m. and 4 p.m. The penalty for missing *appel* was confinement to lodgings or a fine, but there were ways of avoiding *appel*, such as payment to the French doctor for a sick note or bribes for the gendarmes. The gendarmerie, incidentally, was described by one *détenu* as 'the completest system of despotism ever organised. It has some resemblance to the holy brotherhood established by the Inquisition in Spain.'

It was also permissible to leave the town by day and travel a distance of three miles from the gates. For this privilege the *détenu*'s passport (i.e. permit) had to be left at the gate. With some exceptions all had to be back in their lodgings by 9 p.m., and landlords were under orders to report absentees. Many officers attempted to escape, some successfully. On the report of an escape a cannon was fired and gendarmes were sent out to scour the countryside. Officers caught escaping were liable to be sent to the subterranean cells of the terrifying fortress of Bitche.

Some of the wealthier *détenus* and senior officers who were deemed sufficiently trustworthy, especially those with families, were able to live in towns and villages away from Verdun. Some indeed – Lee included – were permitted to reside temporarily in Paris, but the permits for Paris were grudgingly granted and liable to be cancelled for no apparent reason. As Lee writes in glowing terms (*see Letters 21–23*), Paris had been completely renovated and was now the centre of the world for the arts and fashion.

Money Matters: Charity

Many *détenus* had the resources to live in a grand manner. Others were largely dependent on charity. Lee was somewhere in between these extremes. He had a horse and a servant and clearly lived comfortably.

The French Government paid, somewhat spasmodically, a small living allowance to the *détenus*. For those with funds in England, transfers could be made by endorsing bills drawn on English banks through the French bank Perregaux. For those without such resources help came from a Patriotic Fund set up by Lloyd's of London and subscriptions raised by benevolent societies in England. These sums were remitted to Verdun and distributed to the deserving through a committee, one member of which was Lee. Some of the wealthier *détenus*, including Lee, also donated money to help the poor. Those with suitable skills were able to work in the town, but could only keep part of their paltry wages. Loans were available through Jewish moneylenders, who descended on Verdun and charged extortionate rates of interest.

Despite all this there were still many cases of hardship and poverty. Hardship was also experienced by the tradesmen in the town when *détenus* left in 1814 without paying their debts. This was perhaps partly their own fault, since exorbitant prices were charged and inflation was rampant. At one point Napoleon himself had an official warning sent to the municipality that, if prices were not held down, the British would be sent elsewhere. In this, as in many other matters, Napoleon seems to have interested himself in the smallest details of government.

However, despite the limitations of movement and finance there was a lively social scene. The wealthy and officer class soon introduced into Verdun the activities and frivolities of a fashionable English town.

Social Life: Clubs

Very evident in Verdun was the British taste for clubs, where the *détenus* could relax in one another's company and engage in activities such as cards, dancing, cockfighting and billiards. The best known club was presided over by a Mr Concannon, 'who was the life and soul of all gaiety which reigned in Verdun'. He was also an active producer of theatricals (*see Letter 5*). Mr Concannon's club was mainly for married men who had wives and daughters with them. Regular balls were held and there were banquets to celebrate Christmas, the King's birthday and other events. On one occasion 'the whole of the principal hotel was engaged for a bal masqué and none of Lord Barrymore's fêtes at Wargrave could have surpassed it in splendour. Decorations, devices and illuminations adorned the apartments; festoons of flowers covered the stairs.'

Another club took the form of a library, the books and premises having been loaned by a former Benedictine monk, Dom Demangeot. There were over 100 members, who were able to enjoy tea, punch and spiced wine as well as the books.

English newspapers were forbidden; *détenus* were thus dependent on the heavily censored French papers for news of the war and the outside world. Similarly, after 1806 correspondence with England was forbidden, but letters, such as those to and from Lee, were clearly able to be conveyed somehow by surreptitious means.

Gambling

The social scene also had a seamier and more pernicious side, which is mentioned frequently in Lee's letters. Until it was eventually banned on Napoleon's orders in 1806, gambling was rife, not only for the wealthy, but also for the young naval officers and midshipmen, who plunged deeper and deeper into debt. The ready availability of wine and women added to the temptations. 'Scenes took place', we are told, 'which would require the pencil of a Hogarth to depict. Here the unwary spendthrift found an elegant supper, wine, abandoned women – in short every stimulant to vice.'

Sporting Activities

Many activities of a more salubrious nature were organised, including hunting and shooting. A pack of hounds was procured and a smoked herring dragged by a midshipman on horseback took the place of the fox. Sometimes as many as forty horsemen were seen in the field. For those who wanted to shoot, guns were available on payment of a suitable bribe.

But the most popular events were the horse races (graphically described by Lee in *Letters 2 and 3*). Huge crowds were attracted, including many Verdunois and even courtesans '*de haut luxe*' from Paris. One witness records: 'The course presented a very lively scene. The married families attended in their carriages, but the mistresses astonished everyone by the elegance of their toilets. There were to be seen curricles, chaises and four, gigs etc. Every equipage was provided with some dainty, and the dashing beaux visited every carriage, partaking of a leg of fowl or some Strasburg pie from Mrs A or Mrs B.'

Other activities included rowing, fencing, botany, lepidoptery and language study. Lieutenant Tuckey wrote a three-volume work on maritime geography and Captain Molyneux Shuldham invented a carriage propelled by sails which could move at 7–8 mph. After it had upset several locals' horses and run into a farm cart the Commandant ordered it to be banned.

Boredom and enforced idleness brought out the best in some and the worst in others. Duels, which were permitted by the French authorities, were of frequent occurrence and a number of men lost their lives in this way.

Family Life

Some *détenus* had their families with them, some married Verdunois wives and others had mistresses. As one writer records, 'There were a number of women, kept in a handsome, sometimes expensive, style by our countrymen of fortune, who lived with them, as the French say, "maritalement", like man and wife. The wardrobe of some of these beauties would have stored a milliner's shop.' Among today's inhabitants of Verdun can be found some with English names. Not surprisingly there was also a ready availability of prostitutes, with the consequent rise in illegitimate births.

A school was established for the children and for the young seamen, some of whom were only thirteen. Lee was active in promoting and managing the school and in soliciting funds for its upkeep; he mentions it frequently in the letters. A school of seamanship and navigation was also set up to help occupy the young officers and midshipmen.

General Wirion, the Commandant

No description of life at the Verdun depot would be complete without reference to Général de Gendarmerie Wirion, the son of a pork butcher, who was Commandant from 1804 to 1809. 'As great a rogue as the Revolution has produced' is how one described him. And another: 'a contemptible tyrant whose rapacity knew no bounds and who abused his position to extort huge sums from the détenus'. These extortions variously took the form of bribes, sales of permits, illicit taxes levied on clubs, and commission on gambling revenue. He would invite himself to social events and come away with profits from blatantly cheating at the card tables. Anyone who voiced a complaint was threatened with imprisonment at Bitche.

The British were none too flattering about Wirion's wife either. She has been described as a former washerwoman to the French Army, and was known to the British as 'La Générale'.

Eventually Wirion's scandalous activities came to the notice of his superiors in Paris. It is said that an angry Napoleon tore the medals from his chest. In 1809 he was summoned to a court of inquiry, but on the day it was due to report he blew his brains out in the Bois de Boulogne.

His successor for the next two years, Colonel Courcelles, was little better. One of his stratagems was to gain a monopoly of the wine supply and thus charge exorbitant prices. Eventually his malpractices became known in Paris and he was summarily dismissed. To the relief of the remaining *détenus*, the commandants for the final three years were officers of exceptionally good character: Baron de Beauchesne and Major de Meulan.

Release, 1814

The *détenus* were ever hopeful of an exchange with French prisoners in England. For a few, usually those of high rank, this was achieved, but for most it was a futile hope. Lee's letters show him alternating between optimism and deep despondency. Several attempts were made by the British Government to negotiate wholesale exchange, but, according to the British at any rate, Napoleon personally intervened to impose impossible conditions.

In January 1814 the Verdun depot was closed and the *détenus* and other prisoners of war were ordered to move at short notice away from the advancing allied armies to Blois. It was freezing weather with deep snow, and several died on the route. From Blois they were moved to Gueret, and when Paris fell on 30 March 1814 they were finally released and able to return home. It had been almost eleven years since Lee had last seen his family and friends in England.

Permit issued by the Commandant allowing détenus
to leave Verdun during the day.
By courtesy of the National Army Museum.

THE REVEREND LANCELOT CHARLES LEE

The Lee Family

The Reverend Lee came from a Shropshire family, which since 1387 had lived at Coton near Shrewsbury. Their more recent history commences with Eldred Lancelot Lee (1650–1734). He was a barrister and bencher of Lincoln's Inn, and he married Isabella Gough in 1713. Their first child, Lancelot, was born in 1719, when Eldred was already aged sixty-nine. A further eleven children were born thereafter.

A portrait of Eldred's family was painted by Joseph Highmore in 1736. Measuring ten feet by eight feet, it shows his wife, Isabella, and ten surviving children, with two deceased children pictured as cherubs in heaven, and, in the background, a small portrait of Eldred, who had died in 1734. This portrait now hangs in the Wolverhampton Art Gallery.

Lancelot's eldest son was named Harry Lancelot (1759–1821) and it was he who was the recipient of his first cousin Lancelot Charles Lee's letters from France. In 1796 he married Jane Cox, and their only child, Harriet, was born in 1798. She was Lancelot Charles Lee's second cousin. Clearly, whilst at Verdun, he doted on the memory of this young child, as his letters are full of affection and kindly advice for her as she advanced in years from six (when he was interned) to sixteen (when he was finally released). The letters also include discussion about the rebuilding of Coton Hall, which Harry

Lancelot was carrying out at that time.

In 1819 Harriet married my great-great-grandfather, John Muxloe Wingfield of Tickencote Hall in Rutland, which accounts for my connection with the Lee family and my interest in these letters.

His Life

The Reverend Lancelot Charles Lee was born in 1768 and went to school at Winchester College, where his father, Dr Harry Lee, was the warden (headmaster). There was a strong connection between the Lees and Winchester College, since the Lees claimed descent from William of Wykeham, the founder of Winchester College, and thus could enter as 'founder's kin'.

After school he entered New College, Oxford (also founded by William of Wykeham) in 1785 and gained his BA in 1788 and MA in 1793. From 1785 to 1826 he was a fellow of New College. At that time fellows were not permitted to marry. It is clear from the letters that he would have wished to marry; indeed he was actually engaged to marry at Verdun, but the engagement was broken off for reasons given in *Letter 8*. By the time he returned to England in 1814 he was forty-six; and he died a bachelor in 1841, aged seventy-three.

It is assumed that, after gaining his MA in 1793, he stayed at Oxford, presumably doing some teaching, until 1803. Then, travelling in France, he was arrested under the decree of 23 May and held as a *détenu* in France until his release in 1814. Whilst Oxford was his base he clearly travelled much to London, Bath and elsewhere to visit his relatives and many friends. He does not explain why he was visiting France, but one source suggests that it was for reasons of health. His letters frequently touch on his bad health.

From 1814 to 1825 there is another period when it is likely that he was back at New College as a fellow, but no information is available about this period. In 1825 he was appointed Rector of St Mary, Wootton near Oxford, described as a 'valuable living' held by New College. There he remained until 1836, when he retired aged sixty-eight.

He was a popular and respected minister to his parishioners during his eleven years at Wootton, and a generous benefactor to the church and village. He paid for a new roof for the chancel and built a new vestry. He paid a large part of the cost of a bridge over the River Glym and he extended the rectory.

He was greatly interested in the village education and gave a lump sum and the rent from four cottages to build a school for six girls. Subsequently this became too small and was merged with the infant school and the building became the schoolteacher's house. His benefactions, together with those of his predecessor, Reverend Charles Parrott, and his successor, Reverend W. B. Lee (Lancelot's nephew), were merged into The Parrott & Lee Educational Foundation, which is still providing funds for the Church of England school and for assisting young people in Wootton.

Two extracts from the Wootton Vestry Book during his incumbency give amusing insights into those times:

Jan 1826. That the persons who purchase the manure of the parish be requested to remove it from the streets on or before the last Saturday of every month. In default of which the overseers of the roads are to order it to be cleared away.

May 1832. The girls who work at the (church) farms behaved with much insolence to some of the farmers and, being esteemed of little service to them, it was agreed to discontinue employing them.

It was at the same time agreed that no person shall be allowed to keep a pig within the square of the Poor House.

Another reference to Lee's charitable activities, this time in relation to the Radcliffe Infirmary in Oxford, occurs in *Oxfordshire Clergy*: 'It was largely due to L C Lee, the Rector of Wootton, with whom the idea appears to have originated, and Samuel Warneford, who provided a substantial contribution, that beds were retained at the Royal Sea Bathing Infirmary at Margate for Radcliffe patients suffering from scrofula and similar diseases.'

Lancelot's various contributions to Wootton village are commemorated in a tablet in St Mary's chancel:

SACRED TO THE MEMORY OF
THE REV[D] LANCELOT CHARLES LEE
SECOND SON OF THE REV[D] HARRY LEE
WARDEN OF WINTON COLLEGE
RECTOR OF THIS PARISH FROM 1825 TO 1836
THE ENDOWMENT OF THE GIRLS SCHOOL
THE SCHOOL HOUSE AND THE BRIDGE
ERECTED CHIEFLY AT HIS EXPENSE
TESTIFY HIS MUNIFICENCE TO WOOTTON
AND CALL FOR THE DEEP AND LASTING
GRATITUDE OF ITS INHABITANTS
HE DIED ON THE 28 DAY OF NOV[R] 1841 AGED 73

There is a portrait of Lancelot (reproduced on the front cover), in watercolour over pencil, attributed to Philip Reinagle, RA. This hung at Tickencote Hall, Rutland until 1947, when it was sold by auction.

His Character

So much for the bare facts of Lancelot's life, but what do we know of the man himself? B. H. Blackwell in his reminiscences of Oxford describes him as 'of imposing face and figure, strident voice and assumed ferocity of manner'. At Wootton 'he ruled his people as a kindly despot, his memory lingering among them affectionately long after his death. Coming out of church one

Memorial to Lee at St Mary's Church, Wootton.

SACRED TO THE MEMORY OF
THE REV^D LANCELOT CHARLES LEE
SECOND SON OF
THE REV^D HARRY LEE WARDEN OF WINTON COLLEGE
RECTOR OF THIS PARISH FROM 1823 TO 1836
THE ENDOWMENT OF THE GIRLS SCHOOL
THE SCHOOL HOUSE AND THE BRIDGE
ERECTED CHIEFLY AT HIS EXPENSE
TESTIFY HIS MUNIFICENCE TO WOOTTON
AND CALL FOR THE DEEP AND LASTING
GRATITUDE OF ITS INHABITANTS
HE DIED ON THE 28 DAY OF NOV^R 1841 AGED 73

day he found two disreputable vagabonds in the churchyard. "What are you doing here?" "Oh Sir, we are seeking the Lord." "Seeking the Lord are you? Do you see those stocks? That is where the Lord will find you if you stay here another minute." They did not stay.'

The degree examination at New College, relates Blackwell, 'was a farce and roused his never failing indignation. Traditions still survive of his furious protests and the Warden of New College, Warden Gauntlett's, placid insensibility at each repetition of the sham. It would seem, however, that he was moved more by moral disgust than by intellectual ardour.' It was also told of him that he went with a friend to call on a Miss Horseman, 'a delightful old Vestal', well known in Oxford at that time. She was out. '"Who shall I say called, Sir?" "Tell her," in a voice that resounded from the High to Canterbury gate, "tell her it was the man she ought to have married."'

In various *détenu* memoirs there are tributes to Lee's kindness and charitable work. He was a member (and chairman at one time) of the committee which distributed funds raised in England for the needy. He also helped the wealthier *détenus* by endorsing bills on London banks. Captain Hewson wrote, 'Through the kindness of the Rev Mr Lee I was enabled to procure money at no trouble for my Bills. Mr Lee was an English clergyman who, having been travelling in France at the period of the war breaking out, was included in the general arrest. To this gentleman I was greatly indebted for his uniform kindness in always endorsing my Bills. He was much esteemed and respected in Verdun.'

Donat Henchy O'Brien, planning one of his escapes, wrote, 'Cash was always a problem. I, however, procured a small supply through the interposition of a worthy countryman. My Samaritan, or friend in need, was the Rev. Charles Lancelot Lee, Fellow of New College, Oxford, from whom I had at all times great kindness. He contrived now to assist me in my extreme distress by giving the money to Mr Galliers, another worthy Englishman, who had acted as our interpreter. Mr Galliers on taking leave, at the moment of our setting out for Bitche (the infamous castle prison), when surrounded by the gendarmes, cordially gave me his hand to shake and pressed the precious treasure into mine.' (O'Brien was successful in escaping.)

The Reverend Robert Wolfe, who was at Verdun from 1803 to 1805, before moving to the prisoner-of-war depot at Givet, gives some details of the charitable arrangements. 'At an early period of our stay a meeting was held for the purpose of considering the best means of assisting those among the prisoners who were in distress. A subscription was entered into and Mr Fiott of Southampton kindly undertook the superintendence and distribution of it. Shortly afterwards Mr Lee of New College, whose subsequent exertions on behalf of the distressed prisoners are well known, took upon himself at the request of the subscribers the management of this relief. In the course of that work of charity this gentleman discovered that there were many poor children whose education had been sadly neglected.' From this stemmed a network of schools in all the prison depots.

Finally there is ample praise from Captain (later Vice Admiral Sir Jahleel) Brenton, the senior naval officer amongst the *détenus*, whom Lee accompanied on a tour of some of the depots in 1804 (*see Letter 1*). 'I was accompanied on this journey by the Rev. Lancelot Charles Lee, an English clergyman who, having been travelling in France at the period of the war breaking out, was included in the general arrest and sent to Verdun. This gentleman, who devoted all his time and property to the relief of his fellow sufferers, volunteered accompanying me in the expectation of finding many of his fellow détenus in the different prisons and hospitals we were likely to visit. Nor was he disappointed. For many were found and all were relieved to the utmost of his power. The society of this amiable man was a source of much enjoyment to me; and the foundation of a friendship was laid at that time, which lasted during the remainder of Mr Lee's life.'

From the letters themselves some clues can be obtained as to Lancelot's abilities and character. He was erudite and cultured, displaying an avid interest in the arts, theatre and museums while visiting Paris and other towns. He writes in the formal style of the period, but with some wit and not a little cynicism. He was something of an intellectual snob and apt to indulge in moralising. More than once he describes himself as living 'the life of the schoolboy with a man's mind'.

A countryman at heart, he was devoted to his dog and enjoyed riding and walking in the limited area of countryside permitted. Bathing in the river was another pleasure; he was advised that this was good for his health, especially in winter. His health was indeed a constant worry, as was, later on, the onset of middle-age spread. The weather was another constant cause for complaint.

He frequently experienced moods of boredom and depression. In one letter he writes, 'I am sick to death of all things about this place.' This was hardly surprising given that, in the prime of his life, he had lost his liberty, his family and friends and his hopes of marriage and a career. Moreover, for a man of his high principles, much of the company around him was hardly congenial. On the other hand his moods could swing round. From Paris he writes, 'I have all a man of moderate inclinations could wish for, with a good share of health and spirits nothing lacking.'

A kind and compassionate man, he felt deeply the separation from his family and friends in England. (Some of his references to these have been omitted in editing the letters.) He was particularly attached to his cousin, Harriet, the daughter of his correspondent, Harry. She was aged six when he was first detained, and as she grows up he offers high-minded advice on her upbringing and sends her small presents.

His compassion is also shown in his devoted work to help the poor and needy *détenus* in Verdun. He himself seems to have had ample means for his needs and was generous in offering financial help to others. Lee was demonstrably an important figure in *détenu* life at Verdun, having responsibility for the management of the funds coming from charitable sources in England and heading the list of signatories of the letter to Napoleon petitioning for temporary return to England on parole. He could surely be proud of his role in helping to ameliorate the lot of his fellow *détenus* during their long period of detention at Verdun.

The Reverend Lancelot Charles Lee in old age.
This is in Wootton Rectory and is reproduced by kind permission of the rector.

THE REVEREND LEE'S LETTERS FROM FRANCE

1. Verdun, 11 March 1804

It is so long since we have chatted together that I am really at a loss to know what sort of stuff will most relax your brow and least invite the yawns. The very few things which will happen in this land of imprisonment, that teach us we exist, will possibly call forth no observation from you than "it were as well you were dead – better far if this is all you have to say." Something however must be told, since letters are expected to be proportionately long to the distance of the writer.

I shall not speak of myself till our arrival at Verdun. Arrived then at Verdun I found myself enclosed in a small town, comprehending about the space of that iniquitous part of Oxford which surrounds the castle: the river is the same dimension and nearly in the same manner environed with mansions formed for Grays and Drapers, the whole comprised in a few narrow streets consisting of long tall black houses with deep Italian roofs. The ramparts afford an agreeable walk, even in winter. In summer I should conceive them delightful, as they are well shaded with trees. Of these walks, which I have christened by the much loved names of Christ Church, Magdalen and suchlike denominations, I am found at a time when others have scarcely commenced their first naps.

All the vice of London and Paris united (and you well know they need form no coalition) are found at Verdun; these are not represented in any of the fascinating forms which may seduce such unpractised youths as you and I, but after the more gross and uncouth taste of a trading or seaport town. To give you a more just idea of my countrymen's foreign life I must recall to mind that inimitable piece entitled "High Life Below Stairs"[1].

From such censures I must absolve a family whose name is not unknown to you, I mean the Clives [a Herefordshire family]; their house is what you may call a reunion of the bettermost folk. As I become so very old and quizzical that I cannot live by night, I am seldom found at the nightly orgies. My good tutors of old used to tell me "avoid the first fault", since one leads to another. Thus it is with one nightly debauch; it is followed by an invitation for the week.

My lucky stars have given me an acquaintance with Capt. Brenton[2], late of the "Minerva". As he has the distribution of the money sent by our Government for the relief of sailors, he obtained leave to visit the different depots where they are confined. It struck me that this would be a favourable opportunity for me to request leave to accompany him, especially as I had a similar trust from Mr Pnaux, which was to relieve the prisoners from the fund raised by a subscription in England. The Commandant, General Wirion (than whom no man can be more polite)[3] cheerfully granted the permission, Fardley lent us his carriage, a loan most serviceable in this land of go-carts, and out of the eternal gates we found ourselves on February 1st 1804.

Our leave was for a month, our proposed route Nancy, Luneville, Strasbourg, Bitche, Saarbruck, Thionville, Luxembourg, Charlemont, Mezieres, Sedan, Verdun. This journey was not fully accomplished. Pleasure and business detained us so long at different places that we found at Bitche that we had but a week remaining to perform the half of our intended plan. It was therefore decreed that from Saarbruck we should return by St. Avon and Metz. The compass of a letter will not allow all the observations which I feel myself inclined to make. Perchance it is luck for you, since for him who has not the traveller's mania on him nothing can fatigue more than the traveller's diary. My abridgment will therefore be as concise as words can make it. My greatest pleasure proceeded from my companion, whose mind, though nautical, is far better stored with useful and polite knowledge than those of all our far famed Golgothish, civil as well as ecclesiastical, and I am sure I have obtained from it more pleasure and instruction.

At Nancy, the capital of ancient Lorraine, we remained four days. It happened to be the time when the member of the Legislative Council was chosen. The town was extraordinarily full and the doings no less gay. Our amusements centred in the theatre which is handsome and spacious, the acting excellent. This town resembles an English city more than any other in France. The streets are broad, the houses all new and well built, the squares spacious and clear. All the uncontinental comforts are to be dated from the reign of Stanislaus, King of Poland, who as Duke of Lorraine resided and kept his court in the town. His palace is now occupied by the General of the Division; all is changed and the Lorrainers regret the hour that gave to France and Lorraine one name[4].

Having seen all the objects which interest the curious traveller we returned to our inn where we found a note for Messieurs Les Voyageurs Anglais. It came from a lady who, hearing it was our intention to pass through Strasbourg, invited us to make her father's home our home and told us how well she was with the Republican Court and how easy it would be, through her interest, to obtain any alleviation from our present uncomfortable situation. This extraordinary politesse was signed Princesse Esterhinguen. I smelt a rat and concluded that my Princesse was of a tribe which are known to reign by night. I found that she was the daughter of a General, noblesse of ancient regime, but was driven from home for malpractices and was on her way to Paris to trade on her own bottom. Brenton was a married man and I had long since declined (if ever I had been addicted) such illicit connections. Thus had our Princesse, beautiful as she was, offered her goods at perchance the only market where she would have been rejected.

By Luneville, famous for its chateau, which is Versailles in miniature, or New College en grand, we proceeded to Bitche. At Luneville we saw a very curious manufacture from the Angola[5] rabbit, consisting of shawls, tippets, waistcoats etc. 4,000 of these unfortunate animals were confined each in its own cell, which is perfectly penitentiary, allowing no more room than the animal requires to lay in; the plank then covers them till feeding time. They are plucked or pulled from three to four times a year, when they are literally callow and frequently die from cold; each rabbit yields 2 oz a pulling. One would conceive the profit not to answer for the trouble and expense, but it is otherwise.

Before I quit Luneville I should observe that we were present at a general assemblage of all the children at the great church. I suppose there might be from 200 to 300 at the age 7 to 15. These were examined by the priests in separate groups, not only in their religious functions, but as to the situations and rank of life it was probable they would act. The institution seemed to be admirable. Should a church ever fall to my lot, I am resolved on a similar mode of education.

By Strasbourg, a delightful little fortified town, where we passed five very pleasant days, and where we had every reason to admire the humanity of the Mayor and Surgeon towards our sailors, we proceeded to Bitche. This place is chiefly remarkable for its fort, one of the strongest in France. It is seated on an immense solid rock, rising from the centre of a vale; the town forms a crescent at its base. In this Citadelle are confined all those who would have escaped and all those whose conduct has merited an extraordinary severity. The General and Commandant showed us the most marked attention. We were invited to their table (a favour no other time offered to us) and, when our duties were fulfilled, we joined them in a shooting party in the forest, and passed the evening in a friend's home in the country.

Before we quit our military friends the Commandant presented me with a Russian pointer, a species of dog which in this country they call a Griffin. I think he is one of the finest and most docile animals I have seen. I am almost sorry that I have accepted him, as at this hour it is folly to augment affection, and I am certain that I could not part with him without suffering more than one ought to do on such an occasion. I can never think of England without indulging the hope that he may be present at Charlton[6].

By Saarguerine and Saarbruck we passed St. Avon to Metz. As I promised not to be prolix in my journey, I will not speak of the beauty of this country, nor of the Prince of Nassau's chateau at Saarbruck, now in ruins. The salt mines and collieries shall remain uncopied from my journal. Indeed on these subjects there is little for observation for those who have seen the mines and manufactures of England.

At Metz I could have wished for at least a week's liberty; on the contrary three days were the utmost we could allow. This is one of the first rate French towns and may certainly boast of many objects that deservedly call forth the admiration of foreigners. Those which most delighted me were the view from the quay formed by the River Moselle, its three stone bridges and the hospital and barracks presenting a noble façade on the opposite side. The environs are interesting, consisting of rich well cultivated vales bounded by considerable heights. The cathedral is a beautiful piece of early Gothic; after Rouen I have seen nothing to equal it. In the present Prefecture, formerly the Governor's Palace, are a collections of paintings, some of which I believe would have stood the test of the critic's eye. The Library, like all of the present day, is a collection of books from the dissolved monasteries. If this were the only revolutionary change, few objections would be found. The books perchance are better employed; certainly the selections are more perfect.

Our evenings were always enjoyed in the theatre, a never failing resource in a French town. In this the company were excellent. Two sets are well supported, one for opera and the other for comedy. Since the English have been at Verdun they have alternatively visited that town, changing every fortnight. I doubt if the profits from the place are not equal to Metz, though the theatre is not more than a third as large. On their first arrival it was literally an English audience but, as we are given to caprice, it was now more military than civil.

We were bargaining for a Voltaire when a nursemaid and two children passed us that had much the English air. This is so very rare a sight these days out of the Depots that I felt fully authorized in claiming acquaintance. We found them to be Col. Halcott's family, who had by some particular grace obtained permission to remain undisturbed. An invitation to supper was rapidly accepted; you may conceive how delighted I was to sit at table with a mother and ten English children. The eldest daughter was not the least agreeable; her figure, countenance and age might have made an impression on any others but Brenton and myself; from us she had no other than the cold respect which is granted by age to youthful beauty. However it might be, I was never more sorry than at the arrival of the little hour of one which bid us depart. I flatter myself they were no less sorry, as the sight of two English travellers was equally rare to them.

The following day brought us within the walls of our prison. As we wished to bring some presents to our friends, we stopped at a farmhouse by the road, where we bought four capons, a lamb and a turkey. The lamb we brought alive. Conceive then our entrance. Two prisoners on each side, a Gen. D'Arme [gendarme] in the centre, armed cap à pied and at our feet dead Prog and live beasts. In this instance the Scripture was nearly fulfilled; for the lamb and the Griffin (the dog) lay Jig by

Jowl, nothing molesting one another.

I think, my good friend, I have now given you as good a dose of nonsense as ever came from pen by post (if it ever does come). If, as I have written much, I merit your thanks, for the contents I only merit your pity and compassion.

Your letter dated Jan 13th reached me the 7th of March, this was owing to the circuitous route it made, first to Fontainebleau and then to Charlemont and, as we did not reach that Depot, it was obliged to find me at Verdun. Thus six weeks must elapse for any communication, a fact not pleasing to those who love their country and friends.

NOTES

1   A book written in 1763 by John Collet satirizing the life of servants below stairs.

2   Captain Sir Jahleel Brenton (1770–1844) was an American who joined the Royal Navy in 1790. He was captured when his ship, the *Minerva*, ran aground off Cherbourg. After three years he was exchanged for a French captain taken at Trafalgar. Later he was made a baronet and promoted to vice admiral. He was the senior officer at Verdun, and whilst there he was untiring in his charitable work for the poorer *détenus*. The Reverend Wolfe commented: 'His active exertions on behalf of the prisoners of every description were exceedingly serviceable to them; and prevented much of the tyranny which is too commonly exerted towards prisoners.'

3   Lee must have revised his opinion later. See Introduction for General Wirion's reputation.

4   After Stanislaus died in 1766 Lorraine was inherited by his son-in-law, Louis XV of France, and thus became part of France.

5   This is the angora, a rabbit bred for it's long, soft wool. They were popular pets of the French royalty in the eighteenth century.

6   A Lee family home.

Captain (later Vice Admiral Sir) Jahleel Brenton, Lee's great friend at
Verdun with whom he toured the other depots. Brenton's son was
christened Lancelot Charles Lee Brenton.
From the National Maritime Museum.

2. Verdun, 8 May 1804

When you complain that a village in England will not afford a subject for a letter, what ought to be my complaints who am eternally enclosed within the gates of a petty town, situated at the extreme of a kingdom, having little or no communication with its Metropolis, having no library but what may be comprised in a few dirty novels, historical memoirs and polemical discussions of the latter age, no society but our own provincial meetings, no papers but by Government activity and no conversation but what is accompanied by a languor of despair, the peevish selfishness of discontent or the frivolity of thoughtless and inexperienced youth. To such society am I doomed. How I act I cannot say, but this I know, that groan I cannot, grumble I will not, and to talk of nothing with men is not sufficiently interesting to drive the detested gapes. I have no alternative but to follow Dog's policy, that is to grin, shut my mouth and bear it.

To give you my news is therefore impossible. In repetition of my former letter I will tell you that, as summer approaches, we rise earlier, read the Paris papers at English clubs, sign our names at the Municipalité, breakfast and lounge till 12. This is the time destined for those who have permission to migrate beyond the gates. Then are seen horses and carts of every description, waiting at the doors of the wealthy to convey them where their caprice may direct, for all round is one wild waste, the steeps are covered with vines, the plains with sour grass (since water meadows are unknown) or sometimes detached crops of different grains give a little interest to the scene.

The heat must be intense during the months of July, August and September, since the climate is colder than in England till that period and in October the change again takes place and winter at once arrives. What then must be the heat to bring a vintage to its first perfection, which it is in this country, where the wines are esteemed? The natives inform me that they have no spring or autumn. This I can answer for in part, as the thermometer has seldom been higher than 55 till the 2nd of May, when it rose at once to 82 and continued at 81–82 till the 6th, when it fell to 57, and is now, May 8th, 11 o'clock, at 55. After such a change England has nothing to moan at when her climate is compared with Lorraine's – scarcely any settled weather is to be expected till June, and then blessed is he who endureth heat.

Since I wrote the above I have been to the races. Dr May called on me and offered me a place in an open carriage, which I accepted. The course is about a league from the town. 20 louis was given for the use of it during the summer, which may be (I suppose) the real profit arising therefrom in as many years. It is nothing more or less than a marsh, undrained, which in winter is either a bog or flooded. I was astounded to see the pomp and equipage of this English spectacle. Stands, booths, flags – and in fine every sporting accompaniment which may be seen at Ascot, Epsom or Newmarket. Gentlemen jockeys in all colours, horses of all sorts and sizes, sweepstakes, Hunters Cup and matches.

The last of these had nearly been fatal. It was between The Honourable Mr Annesley and Mr Bowles. Mr A's horse fell with him on full speed before he could stop him, after having won the race. It was at first supposed that he was dead. Mrs A. was on the course and saw him fall. She was seven months pregnant. I have since enquired and found that he was not much hurt. He was particularly lucky that every assistance was at hand. Could this be the means of abating the fury of racing? It would not be an unfortunate event, but sportsmen are not of the timid kind.

I have so long wandered from my subject that I know not where to take it up. It was my intention to have told you how we passed our time at Verdun, when the observations on weather destroyed the thread of my story, and the Race I'm afraid has baffled every attempt to find it.

The amusements of the field must finish by four, when a second appel calls us to the Municipalité and the gates forbid further egress. Dinner finished some repair to the theatre, others to the promenade on the ramparts, and not a few retain their seats until Rouge et Noir, cards or dice arouse them from their stupor, and thus our existence is dragged on from day to day, month to month and so on till Emperors and Kings, like Righteousness and Peace, will condescend to meet by proxy and kiss each other. One little misery annoys me daily, and that is the delicacy of the inhabitants, which has prompted them to forbid bathing in the town, and out of it I cannot, as all egress is forbid till the heat of the day makes a toil of a pleasure, and thus I am forced to bid adieu to the river's delights.

Having run through my present life, I think you will agree with me that I am ill repaid for the daily trouble of Shaving, Shirting, Eating, Lounging and Sleeping. If such are the joys of my dancing years, it were as well or better that a millstone were tied about my neck and hurled into the Mill Lead.

I could tell you a story that would nearly suffocate you with laughing. It happened at Nancy, a large town that has a large theatre and large houses, that contains all sorts of things, very much like to Bath, Bristol or London. To such houses it is not customary to go attended; but as I am a man of notoriety, so my doings must become notorious and accordingly (to speak after the shop) the Verger tripped before the Dean – I would give you the full story, but I cannot. I am now laughing heartily at the recollection of it and shall to the day of my death. I thought Brenton would have killed himself when I told him. If ever I meet you, you shall have it and I hope you remember your French sufficiently to allow me to tell it in the original language, as it will lose much by translation.

The Marchioness of Tweedale died this morn. Eleven officers of the "Magnificent" joined our depot on Friday last; Capt. Jervis escaped with the remainder in a boat. We expect every day the "Wolverines".

3. Verdun, 15 June 1804

Every day I feel the necessity of keeping in remembrance "that tho' everything may be interesting to me from the land you live in, nothing can be so to you from that on which I exist". To every object I annex the remembrance of a past pleasure, with sometimes, when my spirits are reasonably high, a sensation like to hope, that tells me "these joys may be known again", and this it is which makes one day tell another.

Not an atom of news transpires from this place. People talk, but on subjects alone which sometimes send the expected respondent to sleep or, should he be quick, a yawn, a note of admiration, or a simple affirmative concludes the dialogue. In these conversations I do not include horse racing. When this becomes the topic each delivers his own unbiased opinion – 5–4, 7–5 etc., etc., on the black mare, Brown Bess, Verdun Lass or Détenu Lad. Such vociferations are heard from the ramparts to the Citadelle and re-echoed from the Citadelle to the Paris gate.

On Monday last I attended the famous Sweepstakes, where nine horses were ridden by nine gentlemen. A booth was erected for the ladies, where might be seen all the belles from the rendezvous of Paris. These are now so much anglicized that I know not, should Prudence or Caprice release them, if they would not share the fate of other domiciliated game, when returned to the place from whence they came, that is, fall a prey to their species. Historians relate "that animals in their natural state can decide by smell, or some unknown instinct, on those which have been subject to man, and (lest their breed be contaminated) either destroy them or deprive them of all intercourse." Naturalists have omitted to remark – "if sterility did not plead an exception."

On this Goose Common course I was astonished to find that the Verdun Jockey Club had levied a payment of three livres on every carriage on the course and 24 sous on each horse. I know of nothing less creditable than at the present day to borrow from the manners of those we live with; let them live on us, but let it not be said that we either live on them or each other. Extreme penury may excuse, or at least palliate, a meanness which, when annexed to independence, must debase the character of the lowest order of beings. It has been alleged as justification that £20 was paid for the rent of the ground and 60 livres each day of the race to the military guardians of the course. In answer, is not the revenue of the members of the Jockey Club at least a million? And a subscription among them might return what sum they pleased.

I have lived long enough in the world to know that it is neither in the higher nor in the lower circles of society that we are to look for those who do credit to human nature. We have at Verdun established by subscription a chapel, a hospital and a school. To neither of these institutions can be found the name of a noble lord, whose winnings and losings are the subject of every day's conversation, and whose immense possessions tend to show how little we ought to esteem the possessor, when no other merit is attached to him who possesses.

This town presents a curious spectacle, an assemblage of prisoners giving a tone of manners to their Imperial masters, a city absolutely changed, houses built, shops established, commerce supported and all by the foreigners, enemies to those who exist only by their residence. Is this not fulfilling scripture doctrine "Doing good to those who despitefully use us"?

My life today is a little less fatiguing than it has been. I have purchased a horse from Sir T. Wallace. It was in possession of his "Porcupine" who is lately returned to England. To me it is invaluable, so much so that, should there ever be a prospect of returning to England, I shall endeavour to take her with me. For a lady it would be impossible to find a more perfect creature. To gentleness, activity and good graces she adds a figure that would in general be admired. Our rides are unfortunately restrained to the limits of two leagues. And the necessary attendance of the morning and evening appel gives to the man a boy's sensation, who is incessantly in fear lest he should neglect a master's summons. When we are found defaulters military guards are stationed over us, number and time as may be thought fitting.

You ask what I think of your taking orders. I wish I could give you mine but, as that cannot be, I think you must do as I do – rest as contented in your squire-like station[1] as I must in my clerical. It is my opinion it would be no less difficult for you to get in than for me to get out. A degree at the University is absolutely necessary, unless you can prevail on some Irish Bishop to smuggle you in under the Church's petticoat. I should think you would scarcely find there the wherewithal to authorize the trouble which such a birth must inevitable entail. As for myself, I may be resembled to the Egyptian traveller who, on entering the pyramid, looked up and saw nothing. "By my soul" he cries "it is just like my grandmother's court petticoat, a prodigious outside, to contain what?"

Pray remember me as soon as this arrives to surrounding friends, beginning at home with the lady, the nurse and the child, and from thence to Charlton, where let my love light on all, for the maids generally used to be pretty. As for old Nick, I will certainly slobber his chops when I meet him. I have had so many bearded salutations in France that no barber in the country knows how to take a man by the chin.

Should Harry be decidedly for the sea, let him not waste his time in learning Latin or Greek. All the world acknowledge the inutility of such a rule; and yet it is followed. The modern languages to a sailor are indispensably necessary. Were you to see the advantage it is to Capts Gander and Brenton, you would be surprised that it should be neglected in naval education. Spanish and Swedish are not less useful, particularly the former.

We have no commissary at present in France. All the business passes through Brenton's hands: complaints, representations, petitions and remonstrances are all in hourly request. Not a Frenchman speaks English and letters to the separate depots must be written in French.

I cannot finish my letter without speaking of my Dog, which becomes faithful and more faithful every hour. He is the joy of my present life. There are situations in which we find the lesser pleasures and attachments are not to be rejected; it is not the time to be too fastidious on causes for contentment.

NOTE

1   Harry Lee was the owner of Coton Hall, Shropshire and the surrounding estate.

4. Verdun, 5 November 1804

Whilst others are busy on the turf endeavouring to make the most of the last great race for this year (and, I hope, for all years to come) I am collecting materials to entertain my friends in England.

The everlasting hopes of preying on Mankind has brought down another set of gamblers from Paris; a sumptuous house is opened, suppers given and genteel women invited. In short every temptation to which poor human nature is likely to give in to is offered under the fairest forms, but I believe the grand requisite is wanting; the length of each man's purse is known and known to be not very long. Credit likewise gives way to distrust and under the existing circumstances it is to be hoped the Bank will retire.

I was yesterday summoned to the Citadelle on a very curious affair. As it may cause a smile, I will relate the story. The Commandant (Gen. Wirion) addressed me a letter under the title of Mons. Le Ministre, a character which I had relinquished since I exchanged shores, and did not even know that my Divine mission was found beyond the country to which its authority was given.

However, so it was and the Commandant began his discourse with a panegyric on the Christian Religion and from thence entered on the duties of its disciples. All this time I began to think of my manifold omissions and of some of my commissions. I was almost tempted to ask him how he came to know the secret history of the inhabitants below, when he put a letter into my hands from an Englishwoman, who had been deceived by her bon ami. The letter told a piteous tale, how she was as maidens ought not to be and how the father denied that he had claims to such a title. Situated as she was she solicited his protection. Having read the letter and said all that might be supposed on such an occasion, he told me that it was his request that I would call on the offender and preach to him the Gospel duties.

When I explained to him that my functions could not carry me so far in England and in this country I certainly had no authority whatever for interfering in any man's private concerns, he still pressed me to call on Sir J. Morshead as Justice of the Peace and, accompanied by him, remonstrate with this Perfidy Man. To this request I asked him "By what authority we could act?" He said "By mine". Then I answered "Let not this authority be wearied like ourselves by travelling; let it not come immediately from the giver to the receiver". To this he had no reply, well knowing that the case was more civil than military, and here the affair ends. The unfortunate girl, I hear, has no other means of supporting the infant than by sending it to the Enfants Trouvés. On the father's conduct I make no comment. I knew him; I know him not. I wish I had as comfortable a conscience.

Of all the climates that this round globe presents, I suppose none is so d—n—ble as this most d—n—ble spot. From a mild autumnal day we are at once entered into the depths of winter. The roads are now hard, the gutters covered with ice and myself shivering before a big fire. Notwithstanding this I plunge every morning into the river and this I find the only specific for the rheumatism. Thank Heaven it has left me.

We have not the smallest expectation of any exchange, either general or particular. All communications on the subject are refused by the Primum Mobile. Here I rest perchance till turned to clay, a comfortable finale, and this by my own folly. Had I been taken where my duty called me, I should regret less this annihilation.

Mr Augustin has sent me £100 from the Government for the détenus. Gentlemen just returned from the race – Mr Mount and Annesley fell – Sir T. Wallace won the cup.

5. Verdun, 2 February 1805

This is the first letter that I have written with the date 1805. It shall contain all the compliments of the season, offered without any compliment and, I hope, accepted as such. Do not, however, return them, as in our situation we can experience no other happiness but remembrance of the past. The present hour brings with it every scene of misery and distress, and the future prospects multiply these calamities.

It will be necessary to enter a little in detail on the manner in which (after Scripture phraseology) we make one day tell another and one night to certify another. When the week and month are told, and I count them on my pillow, I am surprised how I could have waded through such a lingering length and that ever my mind could become so little and so low to be interested with such events as have contributed to the conversation of the time.

To horse racing, hunting and gambling a spiral of theatricals followed. Several gentlemen and some hired ladies undertook to act a play for the benefit of the poor. Col. Tyndale was the Manager; under such a parent I was sure the progeny would not be prolific. The play was "The Revenge", the farce "Love à la Mode". The house was as full as it could hold, the acting very indifferent, except Zanga by Mr Halpin, the receipts £70 to £80, the money given to the poor. Comments are unnecessary. Had it been otherwise, I should have been no prophet.

The poor are now about to act a play for themselves; the receipts, I should conceive, will be nearly equal to the last donations. It is a miscreant set of motley characters, diversified in various ways, and each of the browner or blacker hue. Their first attempt was a piece of their composing. It was sent to me to read that I might decide if there was any expression that could give offence either to the Government or to particulars. I said "To neither" but, if it did not give offence to a well regulated

Government, it certainly did to a well directed ear, since from the prologue to the epilogue poor common sense was incessantly persecuted; never did I labour thro' such a rhapsody of nonsense. It was entitled "Pastime at Verdun". It was not permitted to be acted.

The intended play for Wed. next is "The Fair Penitent", the penitential part being by the mother of five children, in person, make and shape inferioris ordinis commensalis, in language deterioris. How the labours of the night can be laboured thro' with such subjects a future letter must disclose. Mr Priestley, who was confined in Newgate for running away with a ward in Chancery from a boarding school, takes the part of Lothario; could he articulate, his part would not be ill chosen. This ward, I should have told you, died, and he had nothing for his pains but what few men obtain, his deserts, to wit prosecution, confinement, penury and final banishment. In this sense of the word I believe we can boast of possessing more deserving men at Verdun than England herself contains. America in ancient time and Verdun and Botany Bay in modern are colonized by subjects who could not in justice to themselves be classed in any other order or rank of less notoriety.

To speak of the manner in which I pass my life, it is precisely the same as it has been for this year past; the life of the schoolboy with a man's mind is my life. Sometimes I enter society just to forget myself. This like the poor man's dram accumulates fresh sorrow for the morrow. Some few individuals live as the poor gay do in London and very little they are, I assure you, vain to the last, interested solely in their frivolous pursuits. They slumber through the day and show their fine clothes by night, prattling silly nothings till morning bids them hide their furrowed cheek from offended Nature. Such is life for the Haut Ton at Verdun and such their shame.

6. Verdun, 23 May 1805

Mrs and Miss Brenton arrived at this place the 28th April. Brenton has obtained leave to live at Charney, a little village about two miles from Verdun. This he was more anxious to obtain on account of his sister's health, which appears delicate. The uncertain climate of this country will not, I fear, be favourable to her condition. Unless you have been at Verdun you know not what changes mean. On the 17th of this month a storm of hail fell, which rested during 24 hours two inches in depth. The fruit trees were cut to pieces as with shears. The English, I believe, thought of an immediate release, if not the opposite crash, to the uppermost regions. The inhabitants expressed no astonishment, from whence I conclude that such are things of course. Within two days of this severe weather came an intense heat that obliged me to shut my window shutters and to gasp at night for air. How long this is to last the inhabitants cannot answer. They all agree in their expectations of a hot summer, as the spring was forgotten.

Our apprehension of being confined to the town was pretty general, but we were quit for an order not to leave the gates either on horseback or in carriage without a certificate of ill health countersigned by the General. Some few find well the medical staff, others applied to the General for grace and favour, which I did, and obtained it without showing cause. My health would certainly not improve by deprivation of horse exercise. At two miles distance from Verdun you enter the woods and in these woods I live nearly from appel to appel. Here I retrace my life, censure myself for the past and fancy the future different. I will not tell you the fears, the apprehensions, the Prognostics which woodlands wild have caused. These would only prove my weakness or make you as Be-Bluedevilled as myself.

It just crossed me that I wish you would take advantage of your vicinity to Bristol and enquire the Government allowance to the different ranks of French prisoners and what their privileges – accuracy is essential. Also, if punishment follows an attempt to escape, and if the individuals remaining of the same rank suffer deprivations for the attempts of their brethren. Make no reflections, only a simple statement.

The present year has been extremely unhealthy not less so to the natives than to us. Fevers and agues universal. Thank Heaven I have weathered all and never was better or more sound of wind and limb. A little running to corporation, which is the nature of man past his meridian.

The cannons are just beginning to roar the coronation of Boney in Italy[1]. The drums are beating; the guards are conducting the constituted authorities to church. I have not the curiosity to quit my room, tho' I live directly opposite the cathedral.

NOTE

1   The Kingdom of Italy was founded by Napoleon on 17 March 1805, and he was crowned king on 11 April that year. The kingdom lasted until 26 May 1814.

Napoleon as King of Rome. Lee records the firing of cannons in Verdun on Napoleon's coronation day in Rome. From Wikipedia.

7. Verdun, August 1805

The very moment I received your letter I dispatched messengers to enquire after my fellow sufferer, Peter Steven, and within an hour had a close confab with him in my lodgings. He appears to me to be a very respectable man and, at your recommendation and for the sake for his good and pretty wife, I shall take him under my special grace and favour. The first thing I asked was how his pocket stood. He informed me that he should be in need of a little assistance till his bill was answered. This I shall willingly afford. Therefore be under no apprehensions of his suffering from pecuniary distress. He promised to send me a full account of all his joys, and all his griefs, that they may be safely transmitted to his wife. I am to be the go-between on this side and you on the other. Tho' I am but a comfortless old bachelor, I can readily conceive all the anxieties attendant on those who bearing affection with them are far removed from each other.

I have just been informed that the Master of a Merchantman has escaped and that his bondsmen, Sir John Morshead and Mr Elwick, were ordered to the Citadelle. From hence I prognosticate no good to our Captain and to a certainty their liberty will be restrained. At the moment Captains, Masters, Owners, passengers and many détenus are entering the inner gates there to await further orders. Should any further responsibility be required, it will not be wanting for him. Some think they will be sent to Metz, and some that they will remain where they are and some that the more respectable will be released on proper sureties, but I believe no man to be wiser than myself and my wisdom consists in knowing nothing – a very useful knowledge at the present time. The knowing ones are taken in.

Still more escapes. Two détenus have found means to escape the ramparts and go God knows where. They are men of indifferent character, plunged into debts of all kinds and would have been sent away if they had not taken themselves off. No, better not to mention names unless I can accompany with something favourable. If ever I return to my native land, you will find me a new character, an essential part of which will be prudence, and for which I was never celebrated.

Stationary I could never be. Without some peculiar interest in the animated world at home a man must have somewhat more both to do and to think of than how to feed and to indulge his own carcass. This I have long ago found, and I am very certain that I could not have continued to shirt and shave in this Depot of Indulgence, if I had not created myself an occupation. I should really have consumed away with ennui. I have often entered into the feelings of two young Frenchmen who, with every enjoyment that birth, health and fortune could give, shot each other because they could find no cause for living. How often have I regretted that I did not marry at 22! I am now too much of a shelver. Whenever I read a list of marriages, I always look to the convert's age and, when I find an old repenting sinner, I chuckle and say: "Why should not I give joy in heaven?"

You ask what sort of weather we have at Verdun. Everlasting rain. Sure never was poor wretch condemned to such a climate. I do not think the sun has shown his face, take every instant together, for one fortnight throughout the year – cold winds, storms, gloomy heavy blights or settled rains. The glass has always been at variable, but I do not see such variety in the description.

Friends, horse and dog all well. Remember me to all around you – and believe me ever to be your friend.

8. Verdun, 26 January 1806

I have been harassed in mind and worried with a subject that is at all times the most odious that can be discussed, I mean affairs relative to money. It must have been long known to you that I was engaged to a lady whom fortune had thrown with her family in this place. As we were both apparently independent, I conceived there could be no obstacle to our union, but in my correspondence with the family (for they had obtained leave to move south for the winter) I found such provisos that, had they been complied with, I should have been through the remainder of my life both poor and dependent, and in case of a family no authority would have been left to the parent.

In justice to myself I endeavoured to show the unreasonableness of the request and I had flattered myself that it would have been allowed. Our ideas were however too much at variance to be reconciled, and the affair terminated with our correspondence. I wish you to call on my mother and make her acquainted with this unfortunate business. But I beg that neither you nor any of my friends may say a word on the subject in public, as censures must undoubtedly be passed on both sides, and I had much rather that they should fall on me than from me or from any of my friends. I have preserved copies of every letter that has passed on the occasion which, should occasion require, may possibly justify my conduct. But I should hope for the sake of all parties that the subject will be buried in oblivion.

Concerning the living my friends seem interested I should possess I do not believe it will ever come to my refusal. Should it happen otherwise, I will tell you my determination and what I have written to New College – "Could it be so arranged that the Society might appoint a Curate with a handsome stipend, reserving the remainder of the income for the building of a rectoral house (of which there is none at present) and that the College would contribute the usual portion, I would then accept it". Do you not think this a handsome proposal? You observe that I leave to the body to appoint the Curate and the stipend. In case of my death in France the living will be benefited by the whole of the income whilst I possessed it, and at any event it would secure the improvement of a good parsonage[1].

I must now inform you of the very few events which take place in our vicinity. But first I shall drink yours and your little family's health in a bumper of as good Burgundy as ever regaled the lips of a poor banished man. The increase of our miserable Depot has been that which has chiefly employed our attention of late and the expected arrival of more unfortunates is what leads us to renew the subject. The gun-brigs with the transports lost on the north coast gave us many Navy officers, with nearly all the staff of the 9th and 30th Regiments. The men were left at Valenciennes. The Calcutta and Ranger crews are daily expected. Should ever misfortunes increase, a new depot must be found for those of the first class, for thus they are distinguished.

NOTE

1   New College eventually appointed Lee Rector of Wootton, a few miles from Oxford, in 1825. The living mentioned here is probably not Wootton, since Wootton already had a parsonage.

New College, Oxford, where Lee took his degree and was a fellow from 1785 to 1826. From Mary Evans Picture Library.

9. Verdun, 15 March 1806

In a letter I wrote lately to our friend Nicholas I told him I should put you on an active station and that I expected you would stimulate our fellow countrymen in Bath to assist us in a work which has already been attended with the most desirable success. Unfortunately the necessity of it increases every day, but the means diminish. When we first began our school 13 boys and seven girls were the total of our scholars. This was at Fontainebleau in 1803. In 1806 we count from 400 to 500 and I fear the number may be exceeded before you receive this statement. We calculate the expense at £400, to defray which we shall collect about £100 from this place and for the rest we look for friends more fortunate. I am hackneyed in the ways of begging and, should my circumstances be bad on my return, I think I could gain a tolerable living by the active profession of mumping. You can have no conception with what grace I meet a refusal and with what humility I accept the proffered mite. Go thou and act likewise.

Since I last wrote our colony has been much increased by the unfortunate product of the Rochefort squadron. With them we have many ladies, passengers of all descriptions, civil as well as military, and a number of fine lads that would do better at home. Throughout the world I do not believe a worse station could be found for youth, and every hour makes it worse. Gaming increases. Newcomers, instead of being warned by the miserable examples they have before them, flock to the place of inevitable destruction, when it requires but a few visits to make them and their friends regret the hour of their birth. Were I to tell you the scenes every day brings to light, you would stand aghast in horror. What folly! And what fatal consequences! To what degradations men of family and fortune have been subject! And what still greater disgrace awaits them.

All the Masters of Merchantmen have the liberty of the town. On what account this measure was adopted we know not. But

I believe there was a reason as big as a prune – and that not a disinterested one. They live in one house and are visited twice a day. Captain Stevens inhabits a quarter of the town near me, enjoys his health perfectly, but frets a little that he is where he is and that hope is so far removed from him. He must be a good man from the incessant enquiries he makes concerning his family. "Have you heard, Sir, from Mr Lee? Does he speak of our friends at home? All is well, I hope, Sir".

Among our unfortunate brethren of our last party is Captain Woodriffe of the Calcutta[1]. He has made several voyages round the globe, has passed considerable time in the colony of Botany Bay and has consequently obtained much curious and useful information. He tells me poor Barrington has lost his reason, conceives himself Deputy Governor and is in every sense a perfect idiot. The Governor pays him much respect and attention and those who have known him in his better days do not forget the respect due to misfortune.

Mr Tuckey, his 1st Lieut., had continued the history of the Bay from the period Collins had left it to the year 1803 and, from what I see of the young man, I conceive his abilities to have been equal to the undertaking, but unfortunately the work became the prize of the captors. Everything was taken, combatants or non-combatants alike respected, public or private property, everything fell a sacrifice to the avidity of the captors. I could dwell much on this subject, enter into many particulars, which if anything would make a man past forty wonder and would make you stare with all your eyes and cry out "I thank God I am not like unto one of these", but Prudence stops the pen and Reflection shows the inutility of speaking of evils that cannot be cured, but may be made worse.

So I will change the subject and ask you how you like your new habitation, how Madam and Miss [Harriet][2] go on and whether Miss becomes more interesting as she increases in years? What are her studies? The more varied they are the happier she will be. I would not want her to be a blue stocking wench, nor to possess accomplishments that call forth general admiration, but I would wish her to possess them to such a degree as to afford pleasure and employment to herself and respect from the object of her choice. A taste for drawing thinks me as one that lasts the longest and is a less selfish amusement than any other. Every passion it excites does honour to the human mind, inasmuch as it teaches us to receive pleasure from the objects that are continually offered to our view, and I believe I may give this as a received axiom that the mind most sensible to happiness is generally the most virtuous and always the most agreeable to others.

I do not mean happiness to be defined according to the vulgar acception, which sees it not otherwise represented than in noisy mirth and giddy riots, nor in the smirks and smiles of the Public Rooms, nor in the malicious sneers of Tea Table Talk, but in a rational tranquillity of soul, which proceeds from a disposition which inclines us to see good rather than evil and to endeavour to promote happiness by studying to make those around us contented with themselves.

To obtain this I would endeavour to instill a taste for reading, and I would choose myself those subjects from the British Classics, Spectator, Rambler, Adventurer[3] etc., etc., which teach us to perform the common duties of life and make us serviceable to man, as well as to God. These should be the subject of winter evening conversations and of summer walks, which would do away the appearance of instruction, at all times dry and uninteresting to a young mind.

Pardon me for this prosaic detail, which I have been led into I know not how, and which to your joy I am obliged to quit for want of space to be more tedious.

NOTES

1   In 1805 the *Calcutta* was escorting a convoy of merchantmen when engaged by a French fleet of ten ships. All but one of the

convoy escaped, but Captain Woodriffe finally had to surrender. He was exchanged in 1807 and ended his career as one of the resident captains of the Greenwich Hospital for sailors.

2   The first mention of his cousin, Harriet, who was now eight years old.

3   Serious magazines of the period.

10. Verdun, 10 May 1806

I must not delay an instant answering your most welcome letter. To tell you I will never forget your exertions for our poor indigent and helpless little ones is what I can say with all sincerity. Say as much as you can say for me, in the name of my countrymen, to those who have come forward to our assistance when we have most wanted it. To satisfy our friends that the fund in trust would not be ill appropriated we drew up resolutions and I beg you to make them known to anyone who may feel interested in the welfare of those to whom they owe their all.

So little are our prospects of returning to our long looked for homes that everyone is securing the few comforts the place will afford against the summer. I have purchased all the fruit in my garden, as well I know, if it were not mine, my numerous visitors would well secure it against its being enjoyed by those who had the greatest claims to it. I have likewise sent to my cellar a piece of Burgundy wine and have offered to take my lodging at a reduced price for the next six months. This they will not do, right well discerning that in the town I must remain and that, if I cannot change my climate, I shall not easily be induced to quit my porch.

Poor Ellis is now a close prisoner in the City Gaol, with only one small room for his liberty. No court, garden or outlet of any description. His room is on the ground, and that the only one in the prison that is not common to the unfortunate sufferers of every description. Here is a melancholy instance of the wretched effects of gaming. With a very narrow income he would dabble at the accursed Rouge et Noir to improve it. Borrowed of the Jews, he could not pay the debt and was confined to the Citadelle and from thence was removed to this horrid abode. I visit him every day. A scene of sorrow it was, when he first entered, that I never before witnessed and hope I never shall again. The tears of a man seldom fall but, falling, they are bitter indeed.

The hopes of this unfortunate victim are but very slight of being released. His father in law is upon such terms with him as can lead to little expectation from that quarter, and this is the only connection he has whose circumstances could enable him, if willing, to assist him. The debt is too heavy for his friends here; all we can attempt is to purchase the liberties of the Citadelle and, as this must be obtained from the Jews, the success is very uncertain. Jews are doubly Jews at Verdun. I have dwelt more on this melancholy subject as you once knew him and, knowing him, you must join with me in the opinion that his manners are so very prepossessing that in his society his indiscretions are forgotten.

Harriet Lee, Lancelot's cousin, to whom he offered frequent advice as she grew to adulthood during his detention.
This miniature is in the author's possession.

11. Verdun, 18 June 1806

My last letter endeavoured to make you feel how much I was indebted to you for your exertions in favour of our schools. In that department everything seems to go on well. We have cash in hand to continue them till the end of the year and Lord Harwich has promised us his interest towards their support should we be so unfortunate as to remain here another year. When you next write pray send us the names of the good people who have assisted our schools, with the sums each person has subscribed

We have just lost our principal détenu prisoner. When I say principal I speak of fortune. He enjoyed one of the first benefices in England, the Rectory of Lancaster. This carried with it nearly as much patronage as the Bishop of Chester. Mr White had quitted England on account of his health, which has been gradually growing worse from the first day of my acquaintance. Notwithstanding these admonitions he never thought of making his will till three days before his death, and then did not live to sign it. All his personals are to be sold by auction and the produce placed under military security till such time as a legal authority can be returned from England from the heir at law. The funeral was more decently conducted than any I have seen in this country. I can account for it no otherwise than, as Mr W. had lodged for two years at the Mayor's, he was invited and the people are under authority.

Since I last wrote several permissions have been obtained for exchanges. Brenton is sanguine in his expectations. He has received a letter from one high in authority in Paris that "dans une huitaine son exchange pourrait avoir lieu". Gen. Crauford has likewise written from Mortlaix to say that vessels are engaged for the transport of prisoners to England. Would to heavens that this were true! Till absolutely certified I shall not allow my mind to dwell on the subject. Ellis is again removed from the City prison to the Military, where he remains in solitary confinement, removed from every connection with his countrymen.

Poor Gen. Stack[1], who has been confined these two years past at Bitche, has obtained permission to return to Verdun. I like these lenient measures. They look as if the hostile parties are approximating. Mr Payne has gone with his lady to the waters of Plombières. Poor fellow! The last thing he wants is a lady.

NOTE

1 General Stack, an Irishman, served in the Irish Brigade for Louis XVI prior to the French Revolution, became ADC to the King and accompanied Lafayette to America. He joined the English Army after the revolution, was captured and was sent to the prison at Bitche, possibly for espionage. He remained at Verdun until 1814.

*The formidable fortress at Bitche, where escaped prisoners were sent
for imprisonment in the subterranean chambers on recapture.
By courtesy of the Bridgeman Art Library.*

12. Verdun, 10 September 1806

Of late we have been somewhat enlivened by the arrival of Texier and his family. He has read to us twice and has had pretty full societies. I knew him in England and often attended him in Lisle St. It was one of my favourite amusements. Almost all the families have given dinners or petit soupers, where he and his family have been invited. Miss T.'s singing is little inferior to the most admired in London. Mons. T. has great taste on the piano and Mme T. joins in the glees. We are all delighted with them. Yesterday they dined with me and the evening was passed at Concannon's[1], where readings, recitings, imitations, acting, singing and playing made the great hours seem small and almost big again. Tonight the Club give a ball, where they are invited.

Thus you see we prisoners dash away and endeavour to be merry, much more so than our situation authorizes. Yesterday I took my dog out at an early hour and traversed the stubbles, but not with gun. I found vast quantities of quails and some few coveys. The poor dog seemed to upbraid me and say "His former master did not serve him thus". He is now so fully assured of my impotent arm that he does not even look at me when he makes his point. Should this calamitous war last another season (and that it will, and for many others), he will not be worth his salt, as the sailors say, but as an attached companion he will always be valuable.

My favourite mare has for the month past been under the farrier's hands, and this is a French farrier. Oh! They have made a pretty kettle of fish of it. At last I have fired her and she seems to have to have come about again, or I fancy so.

Capt. Brenton had obtained leave to live at a little village about 10 miles distance. Capt. Abercromby and Mr Curzon were with him, but a sudden mandate have recalled them all within the limits of these beloved ramparts. The whys and the wherefores we know nothing about. I have long ceased to ask questions. The females' argument is our reason of the day; it is because it is.

We have had a very desirable acquisition in two families from the south of France. One, Mr Wallers, a gentleman of very large fortune from Limerick in Ireland; he lost his wife at Montpelier in a decline and is himself in a bad state of health, but these are not pleas sufficiently to allow him to return to England. The other family is Dr Gray with wife and daughter. He is a physician of considerable repute and is himself a perfect philanthropist. We wanted such a man and we could not have chosen a better and more useful member of our little community. I am obliged to fill up my letter with these circumstances, which, tho' highly interesting to us poor cooped up beings, are to you of as little concern as which side of the fire the shovel pan is placed.

To change the subject a little – I think I have never experienced a more extraordinary climate than this at Verdun. Throughout the whole summer there was not a fortnight in which it did not rain more or less, and with cold driving sleets. At present we have a hot cloudless sky, fretting heat, such as bids a man stay at home or be fried, the evenings and mornings cold and frosty. All this has given me a pretty strong touch of the rheumatics, which is fixed on my hips, and renders a strong walking stick a very necessary companion. Doctors and apothecaries have told me this and that, all to no purpose. Gray says "Take nothing, bathe till winter forbids it in the river and use the shower bath". This I have begun and am better.

I hope you have seen an advertisement in the papers, which I have sent to urge the humane to contribute their assistance to the distressed détenus. We want £1,000 per annum, and I am in hope it will be forthcoming.

NOTE

1   The most lively club in Verdun. (*See Introduction.*)

French troops entering Berlin after the Battle of Jena in 1806. Lee describes (Letter 13) the passage of the Grande Armee through Verdun on its way to Jena. From Wikipedia.

13. Verdun, 26 September 1806

Well by this time your hopes of seeing me must be done away, unless you preserve a sort of everlasting expectation, which death alone can do away. I am really sometimes angry with my friends in England when I find their letters conclude like the parson's sermon from the pulpit, which instructs us to look to the present hour as but of short duration and to rest our hopes in a speedy meeting in a better world. In vain may we look to this in Verdun, unless it be by a release from all sublunary connections which, as things exist at present, would be an event by no means to be dreaded.

I am sick e'en unto death of all things relating to this place, of French and English equally alike, of all the little cabals, hatreds, dislikes, soi-disant affectations, intrigues, animosities and jealousies. For of such is the sum total of Verdun life. Indeed I have encountered this earth long enough to know that the great mass of mankind ought to be seen at a distance to be respected and that few, very few, will bear a near inspection. He who thinks otherwise, and is condemned to the society of a small town will soon find his error, or love scandal with all his heart and mind. Which is not my case and for that reason, should it please God to release me from this state of purgatory, I am resolved to live either in a great town or in a little village and to shut the door in the face of the person that tells me a scandalous anecdote of anyone but himself or me.

I am sorry, very sorry, to say that I have now witnessed the march of two great armies through this town. The Emperor[1] passed through this morning at 5 o'clock. The town was illuminated last night by order of the constituted authorities in expectation of his arrival. So much oil and fatty matter was lost. The cannons shook the town as he passed through and all the bells made a great noise. What can all this uproar on the Continent mean? Is it the general wish that he who is now the Emperor of France should be Emperor of the World? If so, they who raise new wars do well to ensure him the crown.

In my opinion (and I believe I am not singular) no coalition can stand against the army France is capable of bringing into the field. I have seen above 70,000 of their forces and have never beheld better men or men better equipped, scarcely a man above 30 or 35 or under 25 or 20. Their officers are acknowledged to be the most experienced, to which they have added a real military education. When to this is considered that all honours centre in the military line and that promotions follow merit not money, I fear the armies which oppose them have little to expect, or they calculate on fallacious grounds. Should I be deceived in opinion, I shall be the happiest of men and readily join in the ridicule against myself. Such is the rapidity with which the army moves that carriages are provided to carry them from town to town, relays of which are left at the gates.

During the passage of the troops through this town we are confined within the gates. The political opinions that prevail in Verdun are that France will take possession of Westphalia[2] for the Duke of Bergh and Hanover for England. I hope this may not be the case. Rather let Hanover and all that therein is perish than preserve it through the assistance of such a power. The power that gives can take away.

I am happy to say our fund for schools and other charities is fully sufficient to meet every want for the present year. I will be obliged to you to copy the names of the subscribers you have procured for us, with the sums, and send them to Messrs Lea and Wilson, London. This is done preparatory to our publishing the accounts of the present year, lest we be supposed to smuggle the cash.

Tell me if you have had any shooting this year and what sport. Woodcocks are already pretty plentiful with us. I bought a very fine couple on the 18th of this month for 3/6. I wish I could send Nicholas a few hundred to supply his woods – and myself with them to assist him in providing the wants of the table.

Alas poor Charles Fox![3] All parties must unite in opinion that England at the present hour could not have had a greater loss. What other man in England is known to the Cabinets of Europe?

NOTES

1 Napoleon's Grande Armée passed through Verdun on several occasions. This time he was accompanied by Empress Josephine and was on his way to defeat the Prussians at Jena and Auerstadt. Napoleon entered Berlin on 27 October 1806. Other authors record the fine impression made by the French Army on the move.

2 After the defeat of the Prussians the Treaty of Tilsit made the Westphalian territories part of the Kingdom of Westphalia, a French vassal state. Hanover also became part of Westphalia, which was ruled by Napoleon's brother, Jérôme.

3 Charles Fox (1749–1806) was a Whig statesman and arch-rival of William Pitt the Younger. A supporter of the French Revolution, he visited France in 1812 and met Napoleon and Talleyrand amongst others. Napoleon called him "the greatest man of a great nation". Fox's comment on France was "Its all up with liberty."

14. Verdun, 11 November 1806

Since you last heard from me my spirits have experienced a sad change. I now cease to look forward to the morrow as if it would be better than the present. Experience might have taught a truer calculation, but hope makes no such calculations and, as old [Samuel] Johnson observes, "We never see the superiority of hope over experience more fully than in the frequency of second marriages". As you see, I make weak efforts to be gay and to reason myself with a different view of things, but such sophistries are of little avail. I cannot but see a long, long train of evils falling on my country and this, in spite of my own inclination, is constantly preying on my mind, and my only wish is to cease to live before my country ceases to be free or before she is torn in pieces by internecine factions.

Now I must give you the outline of a caricature that Brenton sent me in return for a letter written under the same melancholy impressions as the present. I was represented sitting by the fireside absorbed in a reverie, the object of which was represented by the prints and papers that were stuck against the wall, viz Great Mogul versus India Company, Berlin in flames, Dresden gone, Retrograde March Prussian Army, Königstein going, Buenos Aires retaken, with many other similar notices and manifestos. In the front are seen a group of Blue Devils dancing on Religion, National Faith, Morality, Charity and Truth. Over the chimney a drawing representing the British fleet upset, and on the wall a large bottle labelled "British Spirits – to be taken when the fit comes on". I confess the satire is good and the receipt most excellent; all I wish is that necessity may not oblige us to have such frequent recourse to the bottle that it will not hold out.

You are surprised I am not exchanged or returned to my country among the many that have found their way there. To the present hour of my life I have never asked for any favour on account of myself and I am determined to continue this conduct to my latter end. I am as well, perhaps better, calculated to bear misfortunes and disappointments than those I see around me, and I will bear them, but not the great man's smiles, nor his polite refusals couched perhaps in terms of promises meant never to be fulfilled. I should rather even that my bones rest at Verdun.

What are all these tumultuous roarings in Hampshire about? And why does such a family as the Thistlethwaites condescend to bow before a Minister for an interest that the very name ought to command? But the respectability of old families seems to be much on the wane. All is given up for the show and pageantry of St James Court, to the necessity of becoming a well-bowing Lord and a kiss my ----- courtly Commoner. From such d----- scoundrels and from all their meetings the Lord deliver me!

Mrs Lee tells me that Harriet is a delightful girl. I rejoice to hear it. Pray caution her against Vanity, the bane of men and women and of which evil they are not cured till they are not worth preserving. The Vanity of the parent has destroyed many a child. In France they are coquets from the time they can speak and walk. There is not a notion or an attitude in a well bred Miss, nor in a washerwoman's daughter, that is not studied, meant to attract notice and the cause of heartfelt discontent if not obtaining praise. I have seen the same studied character in England at a very early age, but I never knew a reflecting parent who did not regret that he had been the cause of the weakness of his daughter's mind.

15. Verdun, 16 April 1807

For these seven months past I have been labouring to ensure the receipt of letters to my friends in England, with what success I cannot say, since none have been acknowledged. Indeed the only letter that has ever reached me was from my friend Ch. Begge, which brought the melancholy intelligence of his mother's death. I have obtained permission from several foreign houses to use their names in addressing letters to my friends. I shall recommend you to use Messrs Mullens and Knox Elseneur. Send it under cover to your friend Capt. Stevens. It is from him I procured the favour.

I am hourly in expectation of seeing my friend and school fellow, Sir Thos Lavie[1] arrive. I think it would be doing his family a kindness to insert it in some paper that he was well at Versailles on the 11th when he was with his officers on the road to Verdun. Our depot is to receive the increase of from 200 to 300 miseries by the removal of the prisoners on parole from Valenciennes to Verdun. The first division is to arrive on Saturday next. I dread recognising a friend at every importation. If it were ever left to my choice, I would infinitely prefer Newgate or the Old Bailey for the residence of a young man to this prison, and indeed I know not in what place his morals would suffer most materially.

NOTE

1   Sir Thomas Lavie, a naval hero, was wrecked off the French coast in 1806 and knighted that same year. He was instrumental in finally obtaining an order for General Wirion to be tried. He was subsequently exchanged.

16. Verdun, 29 May 1807

Your letter is this moment arrived and I am the more eager to answer it, as I find those sent by private hands have not reached my friends. Indeed I had not much expectation that they would find their way across the Channel, as we have always understood the measures to be pretty active to prevent the intercourse which friendship or affection might dictate.

R. Newbolt's letter through Elsinore reached me within a month, Mrs Lee's by Perrigaux in 5 weeks and yours dated 25th on the 29th. From hence I conclude that a correspondence by Messrs Mullins and Knox is the quickest as well as the safest. I have received a very civil letter from their house offering me every assistance in forwarding my letters.

What can Messrs Stephensons mean by saying money cannot be transmitted from England to this country? No difficulty is felt in obtaining it at 23 or 23-10, if the bills are on any house in London. Only give me authority to draw and I shall ensure Capt. Stevens's men their share of the subscription. At his request I pay the crew S.Libre 70 per month and shall continue to facilitate the means of his procuring cash so long as I live in France. He is in perfect health and his conduct is exemplary.

Whatever sums my friends may wish to transmit to this country I should recommend to be placed in Coutts's hands, 59 Strand. They will immediately send it to Perrigaux, with whom they have an open correspondence. I have never found any delay in their house or any difficulty made about correspondence, remittances etc.

As to the vacant livings, were I in England they would be subjects of interest to me. At present I little care for any event that does not tend to remove me from my present situation. At my age the prospects of new connections with professional duties have not their accustomed charms. To be allowed the remainder of my days unmolested and unmolesting is the utmost of my ambition. Were I at home I believe I should accept of

Stanton, as it would be the means of my retaining my present connections.

By this very day's paper I see that my friend Brenton[1] has got into another scrape endeavouring to cut out a ship from the Bay of Antibes in the S. of France. The French papers make his loss 100 men. The professional men hold it to be impossible. He is no less unfortunate than meritorious. It is strange to account for the perpetual persecution that some men suffer, whilst others are for ever accompanied by good Fortune without ever going out of their way to meet her.

My friend and former schoolfellow, Sir Thos Lavie, is fortunately become my messmate. He is a useful and active officer and is of great service to the unfortunate at this and other depots. He was much wanted and, from his conduct, will be no less esteemed than poor Brenton. He has every prospect of being shortly exchanged, a subject of joy to him, but to the friendship much sorrow. He has undertaken a subscription for the wife of Col. Phillips of the Marines in order to send her to England. Her husband has left her with three children penniless. I have betted £5 that he does not raise in one month £76, and from his activities I shall lose the bet, to be added to the sum subscribed.

Poor old Humphries, who had made a competent income at Birmingham and since had settled with his family at Worcester, died on the 1st of this month. He was a worthy and benevolent man, came to Paris to obtain some book debts, was arrested and sent to Verdun. The week before his death leave was obtained for himself and his son to reside at Tours and everything was in fair train for his return to England. His son is at Versailles. His funeral was attended by the greater part of the English – a respect that gave me great satisfaction.

NOTE

1   Captain Brenton was back at sea, having been exchanged in 1806.

17. Verdun, 18 June 1807

I am greatly anxious to inform Col. Bingham's family of his son, John's, arrival at Verdun. He is a young man of apparently excellent disposition, mild in manners and easily advised. I feel myself happy in having been here on his arrival, as it is an object of great importance to him to know the men and manners that are presented to him under so many various shapes and colours. As long as I have the misfortune to be his fellow prisoner, my friendship shall be actively for his welfare.

For several weeks past I have been altogether confined to my bed with my inveterate enemy, the rheumatism. I now walk with the utmost difficulty and cannot obtain an hour's unbroken sleep in the night. I have petitioned to go to Plombières and wait the answer – whether yea or nay I am regardless. Indifference is my present character.

My good friend Brenton has been most actively employed in endeavouring to procure my release by exchange. I forwarded his letter to Col. de Villiers, through the General [Wirion], entreating him to assist me by his interest with the French Government in allowing me to return on parole, that I might procure my exchange with his. The answer was that he had already been exchanged for a Capt. of the Marin Royale taken at Reggio, who was killed in the affray. So much for my hopes, if any I ever had.

I shall make an attempt to go to Paris, for here I am worried to death by the petitesse of business, which provides, if possible, additional enemies and additional rancour. I had mind and spirits to endure all things. I am now according to the sailors' phrase not worth my salt.

18. Verdun, 30 August 1807

I have met with a thousand interruptions in endeavouring to start this letter. Three officers of my acquaintance have made their escape. The guns are firing to announce it in the neighbourhood and everyone is exclaiming "Who would have thought it?" Certainly they were the chosen men of the Depot for regularity of conduct, and for principles none more honourable. Despair will induce every man to take a wide field for a prisoner's honour, and those who are their keepers and their friends should be equally liberal in their decisions. Another officer has since escaped.[1]

Were I to tell you that I am otherwise than miserable, I should egregiously deceive you. And were I to say that I see the most remote chance for my misery ceasing (but at the end of all things), I should no less deceive you. However to obviate every error on that subject I will now transcribe the Petition to the Emperor. General Wirion presented it when the Emperor passed through Verdun. To this no answer has been given.

"A Sa Majesté Impériale et Royale Napoleon 1. Empereur des Français et Roi d'Italie.

Sire
Les Anglais détenus à Verdun en virtue du Décret du 2 Prairial An 11 ont l'honneur de mettre sous les yeux de Votre Majesté leur triste position dans l'espoir que son humanité bien connu l'engagera à s'interesser à leur sort.
Des affaires du commerce, des raisons de sante, ou d'économie, ou le desir de s'instruire les ayant amenes en France pendant le dernier paix, ils ont été constitués prisonniers lors de la Déclaration de Guerre, et réunis en différents Dépôts, ou ils sont détenus depuis de quatre ans. Leurs compatriots les plus marquant ont reçu la permission de retourner dans leur pays, et la majeure partie de ceux

qui restent n'ayant d'autres moyens d'exister que l'exercise de leur profession qu'ils ne peuvent suivre dans les circumstances actuelles, sont réduits à la grande misère. Ils sont d'autant plus à plaindre que n'ayant point en general de rang militaire, ils ne peuvent recevoir que le traitement de simple matelot. L'aisance dont ils jouissaient avant leur captivité ajouté encore a leurs privations actuelles.

Dans un situation aussi fâcheuse ils prennent la liberté de s'addresser à Votre Majesté. Si elle daignait leur permettre de retourner, sur parole, dans leurs familles, ils s'engageraient solemnellement à revenir en France à la première sommation, et ils conserveraient de tant de bonté une reconnaissance éternelle.

De Votre Majesté Impériale et Royale les serviteurs humbles et le plus obeissants

Au noms des compatriots détenus

Lancelot Charles Lee ⎱
William Gordon ⎰ Ministre de Culte Anglican

Ives Harry ⎱
R. Wilson ⎰ Négociants

Frederick Ritso   Jurisconsult

F. Gold   Chirurgeon du Collège de Londres

NOTE

1 The officers had been allowed out, having given their word of honour not to escape.

19. Verdun, 28 April 1808

As I know you are much interested for the welfare of our friend Capt. Stevens, I must tell you that he succeeded in constituting himself a Dane and thus he is in hourly expectation of receiving his passports for Christiansrand. On this occasion I shall furnish him with the needful and even facilitate the return of an enemy to his native country. Whenever he quits us he will have the satisfaction of having left an excellent character at his place of confinement. The care of his crew he will leave with me.

I fear never can I have had as little hope of general exchange. One year passeth over another, bringing with it no other change but those of grey hairs instead of brown, a fretful impatience for placid contentment. Indeed, indeed should we ever return to our native country, we shall be found no less transmogrified in character and disposition than in person. But be assured that I shall call out first and say "My worthy friend, you are scarce recognisable".

It is with a very, very heavy heart that I see the numbers of détenus added. What good can it serve the two countries to retain a few miserable wretches the victims of their rulers' pride? Of what estimation are 40,000 men in a population of 35 million? The evil of supporting so many useless hands ought to outweigh the differences of number, and exchange en grosse would not be to England's loss which, that it may sooner or later take place, is the Morning, Noonday and Evening Prayer of your friend.

As soon as you receive this I'll thank you to enquire at Coutts's house concerning £100 which was placed in their hands in my name, and which I received from Perrigaux but without any advice from whom it came or to whom it is to be given. I wish Coutts to send this through Messrs Perrigaux in his next communication. I am much distressed on this point, as I am ignorant to whose account to place the remittance.

My sister's letter gave me a real pleasure when she

mentioned little Harriet's name as a girl that would be the pride of her parents. I must say you will merit such a gratification, since you and Mrs Lee have spared no pains, and have exerted every rational measure, to accomplish the object of your wishes. The severest trial will be when she is called from you by affections still stronger than those which now hold her to you. You have seen much of the world and are therefore able to appreciate the merits of mankind, but the judgments of a father and a child are seldom placed in the same scale; neither is it fit that they should be. It will be for you to throw in the weight so circumspectly as not to be perceived and thus to direct without the show of power.

20. Verdun, 7 December 1808

Pray persuade my friends to write more often to me. You may easily conceive how desirable a letter may be when I tell you that a newspaper has not been seen for this twelvemonth, and a letter is an event to be ranked among the memorabilia of the place. Were we to be placed at Kamchatka or stationed in Botany Bay we could not be less acquainted with the domestic affairs of our country than we are in our present situation. Of political concerns we are, alas, too well acquainted, perhaps better than the grand operations on your side of the water. Bulletins are not wanting, nor the daily sight of armies on armies to support the work begun, as well as that in contemplation

We have witnessed the situation of the poor Spanish officers on their march to Dijon. Such a sight made the most indifferent spectator heave a sigh of compassion on the evils they had endured and still more for those to come. Nor wives nor children will they behold nor friends nor sacred home. Such was the thought that then struck me.

In my last two letters I requested Dr Mansel, Bishop of Bristol, to be informed that his son had made his escape from Valenciennes Citadel on the 16th November in company with Messrs Boys and Whitehurst of the Phoebe and Mr Hunter of the Ranger. They have not been heard of; it is therefore to be hoped they are safe. I have mentioned the names etc. that their friends may be made acquainted with it. I likewise wrote to the Bishop, as his son had been placed under my care.

There is now a gap of some fifteen months in the letters, during which at some point Lee moved to Paris. There follows a lively and enthusiastic account of life in that city.

21. Paris, 19 March 1810

The account you gave me of your tour through the South made me heave many a sigh. It called to mind former times and pleasures gone, to return no more. It made me form comparisons that I was obliged to banish to avoid discontent. To bring an equilibrium I remembered Verdun with all its horrors. I thought what I was and I felt the change. Content, most ample content, followed, and I wondered that I could for a moment think I had cause for dissatisfaction. Oh I most certainly have none, if happiness be by comparison.

I will now speak of Paris. For strangers this town has greatly the advantage over London. The Gallery of Paintings, the Museum of Ancient Sculpture, the Libraries, Courts of Justice and Lectures in every Science afford an endless source of pleasure to men of all descriptions and tastes. Let a man have a pursuit and he is sure not to be ennuied in this capital; if he is, the fault must be at home. The living, the lodgings and the amusements are all within moderate income. I keep house, have my table served in a manner that will allow a friend to stop in on every occasion and not be discontented, drink good Claret and Burgundy, pay every man his own at the end of the month and do not exceed 10,000 livres a year, which is somewhat more than £600 at the present exchange. I have not a carriage or horses, but I have excellent lodgings in the best part of the town at £60 per annum. In fine I have all a man of moderate inclinations can wish, with a good share of health and spirits nothing lacking. How different would the story be told in London! I have lodgings in a dark court, dine at the cheapest tavern, drink a pint of brandy port and find it difficult to live on £50 a month, which I never did.

The evening amusements are as varied as the morning's. Of these the most in vogue is the Grand Opera, Théâtre Français and Opéra Comique. The decorations of the opera are far superior ones; for splendour and magnificence nothing can be

Théâtre de l'Opéra, Paris. Lee was able to attend operas during his period in Paris. From Wikipedia.

superior. In the triumph of Trajan 500 persons are at one time on the theatre. In Fernando Cortes Franconi's horses perform a charge. In my opinion the introduction of horses is a sad want of judgment, since the perspective is not calculated for so large an object. The men in consequence appear too diminutive.

The ballets are inimitable, the dancing exquisite, the figurantes heavenly, the tout ensemble a perfect representation of a Mohammedan paradise. And were I a disciple of the Great Prophet, I am sure I would be a very good boy, to be ensured the perpetual enjoyment of all I have seen on the French stage.

The Théâtre Français has certainly fallen from its high estate. In tragedy Talma[1] is himself a host. We have nothing like him, but his health is too delicate to allow him to perform frequently. He has not appeared there for months past. Mlle Duchesnoir treads close on Mrs Siddons, but unfortunately she is ugly to disgust, but not all men, since she is now too much arrondied to appear in public. Two excellent actresses preferred Petersburg to the Paris Court and stole away. You must understand that a French actor is nothing less than free.

In Comedy there are not above three or four worthy of notice and these have long attracted attention. Fleury and Grandmenil were in your time. The famous Contat is retired and E. L'Everd has succeeded her with no small applause. When these actors perform the house is more than full; otherwise there are but empty benches. The Opéra Comique or Musique drama is altogether the rage. This never ceases to ensure a crowded audience. To hear a little debutante of 16 sing a song of sixpence it is necessary to purchase a ticket at double price and wait an hour before the piece begins. You see we are pretty nearly the same victims of Folly and Fashion in Paris as in London.

No-one knows when the Emperor attends. This allows me now and then to have a peep at his person without molestation. At the same time I enjoy a ray of royalty from the assemblage of crowned heads. The Emperor is much changed from what I remember him in 1803. Like myself he begins to have the dignity of years, with all the fullness of majesty. I was present a few nights since at a new piece in which his own character was represented, Le Passage de Mont St Bernard[2]. The Emperor was there incognito. The actor must have had no small share of nerves to have acted the part. Nevertheless he played it with spirit, copied the actions and gestures of the original in a manner I should have thought impossible.

I wished much for an opportunity of seeing the whole court of European Kings. This I obtained by being present at a hunt in the woods of St Germain. The Emperor, Kings of Westphalia, Holland, Naples, Saxony, Bavaria, Vice Roi of Italie and G.Duke of Baden with their families attended. The equipages were beyond description magnificent, the attendants innumerable, everything in the English fashion, except the hunting and shooting which, when I describe, will make you smile. The poor stag is turned into an enclosed wood a few days before the Chasse. After the Emperor has enjoyed a sufficient degree of exercise he calls for his gun and the animal is turned before him, when he takes his aim with sufficient certainty to finish the affair.

The shooting is a still-tamer sport. The hares and wild boars are all driven into a small enclosure in which is a stand as on a race course. Here the royal party is placed with their servants, who supply them with loaded guns. The animals are driven before them by the dogs, and the slaughter is immense. The ladies attend and I should think must find the diversion not very diverting. When I saw such a profusion of pheasants fall in the pheasanterie, I wished for some of them in Nicholas's woods. With all these extraordinary sights, these rare shows, I cannot say but I should prefer a country residence in my favourite county, Dorset, and that I might fancy myself happier in strolling over the downs and through the woods with my dog and gun to wading through the depths of Paris dirts, overwhelmed with the multiplicity of brilliant equipages, which scarce deign to gaze to the humble pedestrian.

This is a sensation I am desirous of retaining; indeed I frequently feel I am too contented in slavery. We have of late been much disturbed by the rumour of an exchange of prisoners. For myself I paid no attention to it, but many a man has felt the misery of disappointment. Carriages have been bought, debts paid, money borrowed at God knows what rate, in fine every arrangement made for an immediate departure, when the notes to the King of England's speech said "As you were". I have long made my mind to a certainty of no exchange but as a prelude to Peace.

I rejoice at the idea of your improvements at Coton. What a pity it is that Harriet is so young, or rather that I am so old that I cannot offer myself as your son-in-law. But why not? The Emperor, who is exactly my age, will marry a Princess[3] who is not yet 16. For myself I like Great Examples. In such cases one cannot do wrong, when interest is your guide.

PS When you write again, send me an exact list of the present Ministry. Likewise the Judges and Bishops who have lately been promoted, the great Marriages that have taken place etc.

NOTES

1   François Talma (1763–1826) specialised in tragedy and was an early advocate of realism in scenery and costume. He was also a friend of Napoleon.

2   Presumably named after David's painting of Napoleon crossing the Alps.

3   Napoleon was to marry Marie Louise, daughter of the Emperor of Austria, in 1810. Their son became King of Rome until 1814 and died in 1832. Napoleon's first wife, Josephine de Beauharnais, did not produce a male heir and was divorced in 1809.

Empress Marie Louise, Napoleon's second wife, with Napoleon II, the King of Rome. Lee commented on her appearance while at the Paris Opera (see Letter 28). *From Wikipedia.*

22. Paris, 16 April 1810

In a letter I have just finished to Nicholas I have mentioned my intention of writing to you concerning the future of his younger son. Everet informs me that our old school, Winchester, is admirably well conducted both for discipline and economy and that the Fellowships of New College are increasing to such a value as to make men hesitate to resign them for livings. On reading this pleasing description of places and institutions to which I am ever partially inclined it immediately occurred to me that, if we could persuade our friend, Nicholas, to educate his son in such a manner as to give him fair expectations of succeeding to New College, we would be doing a goodly act. Perhaps the means may not keep equal pace with the wishes. In that case I am very willing and desirous of lending assistance.

Now I must proceed to talk with you on the gay doings of this most resplendent metropolis. Never, I believe, has the world witnessed such extraordinary works composed in so short a time. What appeared to have been the labour of years was designed and executed in a few weeks. Paris has the appearance of another Carthage; all is busy, all is new – streets, quays, squares, triumphal arches, bridges and palaces, all are at this moment rising as if by magic from the ground. It is a pleasant thing to see want and mendicity banished by such beneficial means; seven years since and the streets were crowded with beggars, houses were unfinished and in decay, scarcely an equipage to be seen, none indeed but what was attached to Government. All savoured of the effects of democratic equality, of penury, distrust and anarchy. Today there is not a beggar to be seen in the whole Metropolis. The equipages, liveries and household furniture are as sumptuous, or perhaps more so, than those of our first nobility.

Certainly I never saw any birthday at St James's more splendid than at the Tuileries on the 3rd of this month. It was the day of congratulation. I saw our Cardinal Erskine[1] offering his sacred homage. The Louvre gallery, which had been shut to the public for a twelvemonth past on account of the repairs and embellishments it has received, was on that day thrown open. Immense as it is there was scarcely space for the curious. To see the paintings it is necessary to be there at a very early hour; at an advanced period of the day the sense of smelling is kept most actively awake.

I make no doubt but what you can call to mind the great interest which the affairs of Boyd and Benfield[2] occasioned in England. You will remember that Paul Benfield was the great purchaser of Government loans and was supposed to be worth nearly a million. He died early this month with only £10 in his house and in debt to his servant £600, which he had been incapable for paying for many years. To such transitions is the life of a man liable, especially when instigated by an insatiable ardor for wealth. The Boyds are here living at their ease.

The French Govt. has behaved with remarkable attention to the officers taken at Talavera[3]. About 15 have permission to live at Paris, others at different towns according to their solicitations. Many of the surgeons have been returned to their country. I send this letter by one who was on the staff, who has obtained his passport by Mortlaix.

Our late Commandant (Genl. Wirion) is reported to have shot himself in the Bois de Boulogne on Sunday last. He has been some time superseded and was not much approved either by French or English. If it is true, I hope he has left papers that may implicate two or three of our scoundrelly countrymen, as high in rank as low in character.

The present conversation turns much on the exchange of prisoners and on Peace. I do not much trust to it but, in case the latter should take place, I do not think I shall return to England without visiting Italy, certainly not if I can meet a companion to my mind. I should then like to return by Gibraltar and quietly settle at Bath for the remainder of my days. Such are the present fictions of my idle brain; how far they may be executed time will show. Should I ever return, I shall be known only by name. My friends will most probably be no less changed in manners, ideas and pursuits than in form and countenance and will wonder at my change, unknown only to myself.

I desired my friend, Everet, to send a few books that I thought might please one that I remembered as little Harriet. I send her likewise a little coin that was struck on the Imperial wedding. You will have found it under the seal. I remember, when I was a little boy, they used to make me more valuable presents in that manner. A sealing wax letter used to make my heart leap with joy.

PS Our late Commandant did really shoot himself in the Bois de Boulogne on Sunday.

NOTES

1   Cardinal Erskine, of Scottish/Italian parentage, was educated in Rome and held various posts there. On the French invasion of Rome in 1808 he was imprisoned together with the Pope. Napoleon ordered him to Paris in 1810, but he died that year and was buried in the Church of St Geneviève, now the Pantheon.

2   Boyd, Benfield, & Co. were bankers. The business was wound up in 1799 and the two went to Paris to collect debts. They were detained. Benfield died in 1810. Boyd was held until 1814 and became MP for Lymington from 1823 to 1830.

3   Talavera, a bloody but inconclusive battle, was fought near Madrid in July 1809 between the French under King Joseph Bonaparte of Spain and the British under Sir Arthur Wellesley (later the Duke of Wellington).

23. Paris, 28 June 1810

That goodly dame, Peace, seems ever to turn from the contending powers. Individuals must therefore suffer for what may be supposed to be the public good and patiently await the fiat of the Great. Should an exchange be permitted I shall immediately return to dulce domum, never I suppose to set foot in a ship again, unless it be in Charon's[1], and that will be on a forced mission. My hopes of an exchange, although by no means extinguished, are yet somewhat damped.

Did not the detention of prisoners afford contracts and speculations of various kinds, none would be forced from their respective countries. Of what avail is half a million of men more or less in a kingdom which tolerates a conscription? Sooner or later it will be acknowledged that the maintenance of an inactive population is a scourge in proportion to the numbers and the wants of the country by which they are supported. When interest and common sense are at variance, the latter is but feebly supported.

We have of late been so completely overwhelmed with national fêtes that, if ever it were possible for this people to be satiated with pleasure, noise and riot, it might be at this moment. The fête given at the Princess Borghese's[2] in her gardens at Neuilly was the prettiest thing of the kind ever exhibited. À tout 3,000 people were admitted. The company from the Comic Opera exhibited a favourite piece, dancing parties were everywhere distributed and this, in a garden illuminated throughout with variegated lamps, had, I confess, even in my supercilious eyes, an effect that in some measure realised the descriptive scenes in the Eastern tales.

At the fête given by the Imperial Guard there were no less than 100 thousand people present. The races, chariot and horse, were such as must make an Englishman smile, the fireworks beyond what my imagination could have fancied. Of the banquets and balls I know nothing, that being sacred ground.

Such is the eager thirst for novelty in this place that the Théâtre Français was surrounded by an impenetrable crowd on Wed. last at three o'clock in the evening in order to obtain places for eight o'clock, tickets sold as high as Fr 24. Talma, the actor, and the Royal Family were the cause of this extraordinary concourse of people.

The French can no longer be reproached for democratic principles, if they have any. Neither their writings nor their conduct declare them. Would that they were less visible elsewhere. On very many points the two nations would do well to borrow from each other. Perhaps the best on each side would make as perfect a being as human nature will allow. In neither country have I found cause for reproach on the score of perfectibility.

I do not much like Harriet's account of Phil: there seems to be too much of the sire and too little of the dam. Youth without levity is worse than age with it. Tell me if Harriet has a small watch. It is here universally the fashion to suspend one from the neck; you see the females here at least have the merit at Paris of keeping watch. You must allow me to present one to my young friend.

The thermometer is above 80 and I am to dine at Perrigaux Lafitte's with 35 hot puffy fellows. We have had little or no rain for two months. I hope not so in England.

NOTES

1   Charon was the ferryman of Hades who, in Greek mythology, carried the souls of the deceased across the River Styx which divided the living from the dead.

2   Pauline, sister of Napoleon, married Prince Camillo Borghese of Sulmona. She was the only relative to visit Napoleon in his exile in Elba.

24. Valenciennes, 14 September 1810

You will perceive by the date on this letter that I am no longer gratified by the varied succession of occupation that Paris afforded and that, instead of enjoying the circle of hours, days and months that marked my time without a moment of ennui, I am now enclosed in rampart walls, subject to the visits and restrictions of prisoners of war, counting the days that follow successively, as boys tell the hours that lead to their vacations.

My letter to Nicholas of 21st August gave him a full account of the dreadful fiat which drove all those from Paris who had not accomplished a residence of two years. This was executed with scarcely an exception. My promises for returning were so fair that I lingered nearly a month on the road on the plea of ill health before I reached the place of my destination. In the course of my journey I passed a few days at Mortfontaine[1], the King of Spain's, at Ermenonville the famed residence of the late Marquis de Girardin, visited Rousseau's tomb and wandered over the extensive wilderness which forms the principal feature of the place. This called to mind those much loved scenes of the N. of England, scenes that no other country that I have ever visited can afford or parallel.

From hence I proceeded to Compiègne. When I was last at this place, the Chateau[2] was inhabited by the late K. of Spain's family. At present it is one of the Emperor's favourite residences and may certainly vie with any of them for the splendour of building and magnificence of furniture. The paintings have been chosen from the Louvre. The arbour (berceau), of iron frame leading from the Chateau to the forest, is more than a mile in extent, the breadth 16 feet. The trellis is of wood. A canal is to extend the same length on the opposite side. These works may astonish, but certainly can never please the eye that is a lover of nature.

By Noyon I reached St Quentin, where I amused myself with the busy occupations that the great canal, which has taken its name from this town, has long given rise to. It is now in a great state of forwardness. Various factories are establishing themselves on the banks and it seems that a peace alone is wanted to put them into activity. May this long be wanted! At Belicourt a very novel sight arrested my attention. This was a depot of special prisoners, condamnés aux travaux; tunnelling for the canal is their labour.

At Cambrai[3] I stayed two days. On visiting the Commandant he permitted me to see the citadel where my unfortunate countrymen are confined. They are to the number of 1,200. The situation is healthy and airy, the rooms lofty. 200 are allowed to work in town. Thanks to the generous exertions of their country I do not think they are ill off. From the subscription they have been allowed to purchase hammocks, to double their dinner allowance and to afford themselves medicines in the primary state of complaints, which frequently obviates the necessity of being sent to the hospital. But above all benefits is that of the institution of a school. 300 were receiving instruction at the time I entered. Many who had lost their right hands had obtained the use of their left in writing, and boys entirely destitute of knowledge were fitted for places of trust and confidence.

Before I entered Valenciennes I stopped at the famous post of Demain[4]. An obelisk commemorates the spot in which the famous battle in 1712 was gained by Marechal Villars over Prince Turenne. It was late before I delivered my passport at the gates of my prison and it was with a heavy heart I passed the drawbridge and entered under the gates. It recalled scenes to my mind that I was in hopes never again to have witnessed, but alas a prisoner must be very wise in his conceit who presumes to say what will be his morrow's employment. Having paid due obedience to the higher powers, received my permission to extend my walks to the distance of five miles from the town and enrolled myself as prisoner on parole, I proceeded to perform the duties due to myself, such as obtaining lodgings and boarding.

A Garrison Town gives great facility to these first necessities of life. £2 per month affords myself a servant and excellent apartments, and half a crown a day gives me a better dinner and wine than I shall ever be able to have at home. The town is large and well built. Its revenues are very considerable from its trade in cambrics and from the mines of coal, which are not distant from the town above a mile. The depths of these shafts are from 1,200 to 1,300 feet; the descent is by a succession of ladders, which makes it extremely fatiguing. The water is raised by three or four pumps, as occasion may require. These force the water into each other until it meets the summit.

The environs are almost on a level, affording little to entertain the eye. The cultivation is corn and poppy. Our walks are frequently to the Duke of York's tree, the British lines in 1793[5]. From hence we can trace the plan of attack. The town suffered severely; many of the streets are still in ruins. The cathedral scarcely affords a vestige of its former greatness, and I do not believe there is one house in town that has not been roofed since this memorable siege.

The English confined in the Citadel are about 1,000. The situation is low and the area not sufficiently extensive. 300 have permission to work in town on giving up the French allowance of money, consisting of six farthings per day. If they sleep in town, they have no claim for provisions. The price of labour, be it what it may, is 15 sols or seven pence ha'penny per day. The prisoners on parole are nearly 40 in number; of these from 20 to 30 were sent from Paris by the last decree.

I entrusted two watches to a lady of my acquaintance who left France early in August. These I addressed to my sister requesting her to forward one to Harriet. They are not worn in France with seals, neither have they the honour of an inner berth. The French ladies of family are far more decently dressed than the English. We are notorious for caricaturing fashions. An English lady in Paris certainly appears to be what her friends would wish her not to be.

Thank you very much for your idea of benefices and appendages. I am too old and too indolent and too much inclined to freedom of body and mind to become active either in one state or the other.

The remainder of my life will be devoted to summer wanderings (whilst health permits) and winter perchings in Bath or elsewhere. But heaven only knows when these wanderings will be allowed. Day after day do we eagerly take up the Govt gazette, thinking to see some favourable paragraph for an exchange, but find none. A Paris post engages all our attention and every man addresses his acquaintance with "What say your letters today?" Our hopes are, however, much on the wane. Our fears keep us tremblingly alive.

We have just heard of the taking of Almeida[6]. I tremble for our Army. After the folly of sending it to Spain the wisest course will be to ensure its return, which will require more activity than was shown on some expeditions.

NOTES

1 Bought by Joseph Bonaparte in 1798, the chateau is now a hotel.

2 The Château de Compiègne had been a royal residence since 1374. In 1804 Napoleon commissioned major alterations to the chateau and gardens.

3 Cambrai suffered badly under the Terror. Most of the religious buildings, including the cathedral, were demolished. It was the Duke of Wellington's headquarters for the army of occupation from 1815 to 1818.

4 This is a misspelling of Denain, the site of a battle of the Spanish War of Succession. Here in 1712 the French defeated the combined forces of the Dutch and Austrians.

5 In 1793 Valenciennes was captured and plundered by Anglo-Austrian forces under the Duke of York and the Prince of Saxe Coburg. It was retaken by the French in 1794.

6 In 1810 a small force of 5,000 under General Cox was besieged in Almeida in Portugal by 14,000 soldiers under Marshal Ney. A freak shell caused the gunpowder store to explode, and General Cox was forced to capitulate.

25. Verdun, 5 April 1811

There was a time when it would have been a subject of great joy to me to have found myself so near to all the preferment that New College has to give. As it is, I feel no more interest in it than in the succession of the Canons of St Denis or the promotion of the Imperial Bishops, and indeed it is to me of little more import, as I hope and trust that I shall never be found sufficiently foolish to domiciliate myself in Parish retirement, searching for happiness in the plenitude of my coffers or purchase a wife at the expense of comfort and common sense. In days of yore I had conceived no joys separate from such a state, and so I still think for youth. But when an old man fancies a helpmate a necessary appendage he too frequently pleases his eye, and then farewell to all his Châteaux en Espagne.

I wish I could tell you what are my pleasures; I should then be able to write on some pleasing subject, but alas such is our present state that even hope will not bring a delusive joy. Sometime I dare to fancy the return of the St Domingo Army[1] may lead to change and that one government, not wishing to be outdone in generosity by the other, may say to the Riff Raff Rabble détenus "Get you gone, you dirty dogs". The Go would not be considerable either in number or value, but it would be a very good Go for me.

Despair has induced many an unfortunate to attempt his escape. The frequency of the act has induced the Government to put in force an obsolete law which punished the accused with six years' labour. Many have incurred this severe penalty and among them some worthy men. I hope we shall have too much humanity to attempt retaliation, by which the innocent become victims and the guilty smile at unavailing anger. Generosity will gain its object when revenge increases the evil it wishes to diminish. Let England continue to diminish the number of unfortunate sufferers at home, and at least she will have the satisfaction of having offered an example worthy of following and which sooner or later will be followed.

Give my love to Harriet. I long to see her – and likewise all the improvements you are making to the Hall, which can never please the eye while the Chapel remains. I cannot see your objection to pulling it down, when our ancestors are removed. The endowment I would add to the Parish living. The example the family affords in attending the public Church is of more avail than all the pomp and pride of select demi-private worship. I love community of prayer, the dress of Sunday and the cheerfulness of devotion and, had I a Parish, I would encourage after service rural games and at noon the merry dance. I am convinced no good was ever yet obtained from the indolent inactivity of the Presbyterian Sabbath, and I am convinced the devout much mistake the meaning of "Thou shalt do no work". Both men and maidens have cause to sorrow for idle hours, and the parish too, but not the Pot-House.

NOTE

1 The slave army in Haiti that rose up and, despite the best efforts of Napoleon, defeated the French, resulting in Haitian independence in 1804.

26a. Verdun, 25 October 1811

How did I envy you when I read the account of your little parties, as well as your journeys into Shropshire. When shall I partake of such heartfelt satisfaction or even speculate on the probability that such domestic delights are ever again to be experienced? Never, I verily believe. Here I must lingering live and in that case most joyfully die. To a certainty these last eight years have made an atonement for the peccadillos of former days, however numerous they may have been or whatever their character.

I very easily enter into your feelings on the subject of Coton[1]. The advantage of parting with it is obvious in the point of revenue but, supposing Harriet should choose some younger son, with only a funded or lifehold property (for affection is not always in the ratio of acres), with what regret would you see your hereditary property alienated from your family? Besides, my good friend, in these very extraordinary and, I may say, perilous times landed property is the safest tenure. Whatever may happen, if a man does not forsake his land, the chances are his land will remain with him. As to other possessions, credit gives it the value; the want of it takes it away.

Your plan concerning the chapel I admire and the sooner the old one is removed the better. The Brewhouse can be consecrated whenever you can procure the Bishop's blessing. It may be chapelised, as circumstances admit. You do not want the pomp of prayer. The object is to secure the endowment to the Alvely Rector, for he has but a scanty pittance. I hope and trust the old Coton will remain with you in your time and that it may have charms to retain a resident squire in your family for ages yet to come. If not resident, I am indifferent as to the possessor. A Squire and a Parson may do an infinity of good by their presence, and the Parish never fails to testify what evils their absence creates.

I believe I mentioned in a former letter that it was my intention to use every interest toward procuring my return to Paris. This I have fortunately effected for three months, and I hope I shall be able to prolong. I purpose leaving this place on the 7th and calculate on arriving at Paris on the 10th, where this letter will be finished.

Those who have not been confined within rampart walls and doomed to all the uninteresting detail of depot conversations can little appreciate the sensations which even a temporary absence occasions. I do assure you I feel them in full force at this moment. No schoolboy ever calculated the hours which detained him from dulce domum more accurately than I do those which hold me within these walls. At 43 a man (not military) has a right to calculate on being free from the miseries of detention, but fate designed otherwise for me. My years of expectation have been consumed in all the bitterness of thralldom. As to the concluding years it little matters on which soil they are finished. The same portion of earth will be allowed me, and whether the bell tolls or not je ne m'en soucie guère. All I dare hope for is to be free from Depot rules and prisoners' dialect.

Adieu; the continuation at Paris.

NOTE

1   Coton Hall, Harry Lee's country house. His only daughter, Harriet, inherited it, but after her marriage to John Wingfield the house and estate was sold.

26b. Paris, 5 December 1811

At length settled in this fascinating place I feel, as I may say, a new being. Conversation, manners, acquaintance all new or renewed – no ennui. With the day occupation follows for its employment and, when this happens, a man cannot be said to be unhappy. At least it is his own fault if he is, health and a decent maintenance granted him. My permission to leave the depot of Verdun was obtained through the interest of a French Officer (Capt. Muller), who was long a prisoner in England, chiefly at Montgomery and, having received some attentions from the family of a friend, has been unremitting in his exertions towards obtaining for me this essential favour. Neither could he have succeeded in his object, had he not been personally acquainted with the Minister of War.

Now, I could wish my friends in England (should it lay in their power) to assist me in showing that I am not insensible to the obligations and I know no other way they can do it than by the civilities they might show to M. Widman (a friend of Capt. Muller) now a prisoner at Brecknock. He commanded a gunboat. Perhaps you may meet some good Welshmen in Bath who have acquaintance in that town. If you do, I entreat you to recommend M. Widman to their notice for my sake. Should it be my fortune to return to England before him, I will not rest before I procure his release. It will be hard, very hard, if I cannot, amongst all my ci-devant connections, collect sufficient interest to send one Unfortunate home. If I cannot, it might be as well for me to remain where I am.

I have just received a charming remembrance from your charming daughter, Harriet, which I will acknowledge by the very first opportunity. These little tokens of affection and friendship bid all the thoughts of kindred and home rush to my mind and, like the sight of gold to a penniless wretch, which makes him doubly poor, I become more miserable from the reflection of what I have lost.

I am very greatly obliged to Mr A. Lee for his exertions in my favour, but they are useless. He might as well attempt to procure me a succession to the throne of England as my release for even three months. And indeed, if offered for that time, I hope I would have the firmness to refuse it. The pain of returning would far exceed the pleasure a temporary return could procure.

By some ladies who are expecting their passports to England I have sent two Angola shawls, which I beg Mrs Lee and Miss Horseman to throw over their shoulders on a cold winter's day in remembrance of me. They are not remarkable elegant, but they are remarkable useful, and as such may be borne with. I am told they are not very common in London. This induces me to send them. If otherwise, please excuse me.

27. Paris (Hotel d'Avranche, Rue Gerutti), 10 May 1812

I have now another petition before the Minister of War, my leave being renewed every three months, and my lease expires on the 15th. I am in hopes it will be continued, but I cannot but be nervous at the expiration of each term.

I have received a letter from Mr Widman, who is now at Montgomery. I wish I had sufficient interest to get him home – I think I ought. It is but a small request to ask for the release of a Lieut., totally unprotected in this country, without property or connexions. If I could do it, I would cheerfully advance him wherewithal to rejoin his family. Most of my acquaintances have found means to obtain similar favours. Wolfe has returned two or three, Crespigny a Capt., Forbes a Major, Hazlefoot a Lieut., these within my knowledge, but there are many more instances of similar favours accorded by our Government.

Pray desire Duncan to send Harriet my set of Gilpin's works. I think they will amuse her and may tend to form a taste, which will eventually be the source of many an hour's satisfactory amusement. It is with this in view that I must beg of you to take from my New College store whatever books and drawings you and the Duncans agree may either amuse or instruct my almost unknown friend. Yet from what I have heard from those who discern she is as interesting to me as if my acquaintance had never been interrupted. For I have friends on whose judgment I can rely better than on my own, and I never fail to enquire about those who ought naturally to interest me. Do not scruple to comply with my request. The obligation on your part will not be much in taking from me that which can be of no use to me, and in knowing I can in any way be of service to Harriet I shall be amply repaid.

28. Paris, 13 July 1812

I sent to Mrs H. Lee my portrait, which is generally esteemed like, though somewhat too grave in character. I am sitting for another; should the manufacture succeed, I design it for your dressing room. I believe it is all you are likely to see of the original.

By the by, I really ought to apologise for sending such shabby concerns as those Angola shawls. The object I had in view was that of procuring my friends a little homely warmth. And I was told that the Angola fur was not easily procured in England. If it is, I ought to be ashamed of myself. I beg pardon, but I meant well.

By Mrs Lee I send my friends, the Duncans, "The Mineralogy of the Environs of Paris", a work in high estimation, with Dr Gall's late publication, a work in much esteem. You will find enclosed some parcels of seeds of the Arbor Judée (Judas Tree). I do not recollect having seen it in England and I recommend the cultivation of it. It is a hardy genus and I should think would suit our climate, as it flourishes in Paris.

Also enclosed are engravings of the Emperor and Empress for Mr A. Lee, should he still be with you. I was told he wished to procure good likenesses; these are the best. The Empress is much changed since her marriage. I saw her a few nights since at the Opera. She appeared to me much emaciated; the embonpoint she brought with her from Vienna was totally gone. The Emperor on the contrary becomes lustier every day.

The Racing Calendar from Verdun will show you how sorrow can be forgotten, how avarice will level all ranks and how anxious we are of exposing ourselves to the natives by translating our follies even into their language. The Exposition of the Athenée, which I have likewise enclosed, will show you what an excellent society is established in Paris, which admits anyone that is presented by a known member at the moderate price of £5 per annum.

There were to be two more years of internment for Lancelot Charles Lee until his release in 1814, but no further letters survive.

BIBLIOGRAPHY

John G. Alger, *Napoleon's British Visitors and Captives, 1801–15* (London, 1904)

Captain Edward Boys, *Narrative of a Captivity, Escape and Adventures in France and Flanders during the War* (London, 1817)

Edward Fraser, *Napoleon the Gaoler* (1914)

Captain M. Hewson, *Escape from the French* (edited by Antony Brett-James, London, 1981)

Richard Langton, *Narrative of a Captivity in France from 1809 to 1814* (London, 1836)

James Henry Lawrence, *A Picture of Verdun from the Portfolio of a Detenu* (London, 1810)

Michael Lewis, *Napoleon and His British Captives* (London, 1962)

Donat Henchy O'Brien, *My Adventures during the Late War* (London, 1814)

Reverend Henry Raikes, *Memoir of the Life and Services of Vice-Admiral Sir Jahleel Brenton, Baronet, K.C.B.* (London, 1846)

Reverend R. B. Wolfe, *English Prisoners in France* (1830)